Stories and Fables from the Mahabharata

Stories and Fables from the Mahabharata

Dr. R.K. Sinha

Ocean Books Pvt. Ltd.

ISO 9001:2008 Publishers

Published by
Ocean Books (P) Ltd.
4/19 Asaf Ali Road,
New Delhi-110 002 (INDIA)
e-mail: info@oceanbooks.in

ISBN 978-81-8430-385-8
STORIES AND FABLES
FROM THE MAHABHARATA
by Dr. R.K. Sinha

Edition
First, 2016

Price
₹ 250.00 (Rupees Two Hundred Fifty only)

Printed at
R-Tech Offset Printers, Delhi

To

My American Grandchildren

Dhruv, Dheer, Radhika

Preface

The Mahabharata is the "book of books". It is an encyclopedia of ancient Bharat (India). That is why it is said, "What is not in the Mahabharata is not in Bharat (India)". Expanse and depth of thoughts and ideas in this book are bewildering, The highest and lowest of human nature are painted in glowing colors. The stories of gods, men, demons, birds, beasts, insects and plants are spread on a big canvas. Conflicts of emotions and call of duty, the wisdom and foolishness of human endeavors described in the Mahabharat, stun the readers. The variety of characters and situations are perennial source of inspiration for politicians, poets, writers and scholars. Even for saints and sages.

The Mahabharata is full of interesting and instructive fables. Much before the Aesop's fables, and the Panchtantras, the Mahabharata presented gems of political, diplomatic and humanitarian thoughts and ideas through the fables. They are used to impart valuable ethical and social lessons.

Life forces are indivisible. The vibration of love, hatred, fear, sincerity, and sacrifices are observed in all species of life. Even plants and animals are supposed to understand and respond to the love and hatred of human beings. The Vedant sees the same spirit pervading through the entire universe. From this non-dualism springs the concept of reverence for life. But the absolute truth of philosophy has to contend with the practical realities of life. In the struggle for existence, practical tips and examples are required, to sail smoothly through the difficult waters of life's struggles.

Nothing can serve this purpose better than the fables. The fables from the Mahabharata provide us practical knowledge and also elevate us to higher ethical standards.

I hope the readers will enjoy the stories to the full, and that will be the real reward for the writer.

—Dr. R.K. Sinha

Contents

FABLES FROM THE MAHABHARATA

STORIES FROM THE MAHABHARATA

Humiliation of Draupadi in the Open Court

When under a conspiracy, Duryodhana planned to reinvite the Raja Yudhishthira for a game of dice. Yudhisthira had this weakness of dice playing. He could not resist the temptation of the game. Vidur dissuaded him and all his friends and well-wishers wanted him to reject the offer of the friendly game of dice at the court of Hastinapur. Yudhishthira reached there to play the dice. Duryodhana appointed Shakuni to play the dice on his behalf. Yudhishthira started putting his valuable things on the stake. Shakuni was a cunning fellow, he was expert in cheating in the game. So one by one, he won everything. Ultimately, Yudhishthira put his brothers on the stake. Shakuni won it. Then he put his ownself on the stake of dice, Shakuni won it with a sleight of hand. Now even Draupadi was put on stake and she was won by Shakuni. Duryodhana asked Dushasan to bring Draupadi in the open court. At that time she was under

one piece of cloth. She was dragged to the open court of dice. Vidur had warned of the bad consequences of the game. He pleaded the King Dhritarashtra to control his son's greed. At this there was argument between Duryodhan, and Vidur. Ultimately Draupadi was dragged to the open court by Dushasan. The entire court, Bheeshma, Dronacharya, Kripacharya, kept silent and did not respond to save the honour of Draupadi. They didn't even speak a word in her defence. Ultimately, Draupadi started praying Lord Krishna for saving her honour. In the meantime, she made an appeal to Bheeshma to speak in her favour but Bheeshma didn't. Lord Krishna arrived at the scene and when Dushasan tried to make Draupadi naked by pulling out the cloth, Lord Krishna supplied so much of cloth that they could not uncover her body. Duryodhan was very angry with Draupadi. When Duryodhan had visited the Indraprastha Palace of Draupadi, the art of the floor at the house was dazzling. Duryodhan tried to pass the gate, but there was no door. He lifted his cloth to cross the water but there was no water. So Draupadi commented that the son of a blind man is himself a blind man. At many occasions, he wanted to possess Draupadi but he had failed in his scheme. Thus, Lord Krishna saved Draupadi's honour in the open dice court of the Kaurvas. After this dice play the Pandavas were to go for *Vanvas* for 12 years.

And there was a condition that in the last one year they were not to be discovered by anybody. If they were discovered they'll have to spend another twelve years in the forest. So this game of dice was watershed in the story of Mahabharata.

❑

The Obedient Students

There was a famous maharishi named Ayodhomya he had students in his ashram, Manu, Aruni, Panchal and ved. One day, the maharishi sent Aruni to his field and said please go and repair the broken fences. Aruni, at the orders of his master, went to the farm and started repairing the broken fences but could not succeed. So he thought that he should lie on the broken place to block the flow of water and he did so. By evening, he did not return to the *ashram* so the master with his other students went to search for him. He found him lying on the broken fence and blocking the water from flowing from the field. The master came to the farm and shouted for Aruni. So he got up from the broken fence and said "I am here". He bowed to the feet of the *guru* and said "what next duty is to be performed by me". The *guru* replied "you have stood up from the broken fence of the farm so now on you will be called Uddalaka and you have followed my orders so all the law of *dharma* will flash in your mind". Aruni was very happy and he was obliged and then he left for his home. Another student was Upamanyu. He

was assigned the duty of looking after the cows of the *ashram*. Every evening he would come back after grazing the cows and stood up before the *guru* and touch his feet. One day *guruji* said, Upamanyu you are looking very stout and strong, what food do you live on?" He said I live on begging alms. The *guru* said you should not live on your alms without offering that to me. Now the *guruji* used to collect all the alms for himself and did not give anything to him. Even then he would daily come and touch the feet of the *guru*. One day *guruji* asked, I take all the alms aways from you still you are stout and strong, what do you live on? He said after you take my first alms, I go on another begging and live on that. The *guruji* said this is against the code. You should not do that. This will harm the interest of other students who go to beg for food. He stopped begging second time, still he would come daily to his teacher and bow to his feet. One day, the *guru said,* I have taken all the alms begged by you, how do you live and remain so strong? He said I live on cows' milk. Guruji said you have no permission to take cows' milk. Again after some days, the *guruji* said, how do you survive now? He said I live on milk which calf throw out from their mouth. *Guruji* said that the calf throw their milk to you out of kindness. Now all the venues of food were stopped for him. He was very hungry so he chewed the leaves of a poisonous plant and he was blind and fell in a well in the forest. *Guruji* with his students came to search for him and called out his name Upamanyu. He said, I have fallen in a well as I became blind. Then the *guru* asked him to pray for Ashwini Kumar, the doctors heavenly gods. He prayed to them and they appeared. They offered a sweet bread to him and said that take it and your eyesight will be back. Upamanyu said that sir, I must take permission of my *guru* to take this. Ashwini Kumar said, your *guru* had taken the bread, in similar circumstances without taking the permission of his *guru*. He insisted on the permission of his *guru* and only on the permission took the sweet bread. Ashwini kumar blessed him that all the shastras will flash to his mind automatically. Ved was the third student. *Guruji* said Ved I am going out of my house, you stay in my house and look after them. For a long time, he looked after the affairs of the *guru* in his house, like a bull he used to carry chores of the family. In all circumstances, he was always happy. Then *guru* was happy with him and he gave him the knowledge of the vedas. After the permission of the *guru*, the convocation was held and he was permitted to be a householder. He had three students with him, but he never ordered them to do service of work or to do any other work, because he knew the hardships students faced at the house of the *guru*. Uttanka was his famous student.

❑

The Invisible Queen to Person with Unclean Mouth

Acharya Ved had a student called Uttanka. He was devoted to his teacher. Once the teacher was going out, he said to Uttanka that if there was any need, you were fulfil it. Having said this the *guru* went out. One day, the women of the household called Uttanka and said, the wife of your teacher is under *ritukaal* and the teacher is not inside the house. I will not do anything by the dictate of women. Guruji has not given me any such orders. After sometime the Acharya returned and he was reported about Uttanka. He called Uttanka and said, now I am very happy with you. Now I'll permit you to finish your education and go home. Then Uttanka said, I want to give some *gurudakshina*. The *guru* kept silent and asked him to stay for some more time. After some time he again insisted on knowing the nature of *gurudakshina*. So one day *Acharya* said, ask this from the *gurupatni*. The student went to *gurupatni*, who said, the king Paupya's wife has two earrings, and I want those. After four days a Vrat called Punya was to

be celebrated. She wanted to perform the *Vrat* by wearing these two earrings and feed the Brahmins. When Uttanka heard this, he set on the journey to the palace of King Paupya. On the way, he saw somebody riding a bullock. He told him, to eat the dung of this bullock, and Uttanka did so. In a hurry, he could not wash his mouth properly. Uttanka reached the palace and saw the king sitting on his throne. He told the king, your lordship, I have come here as a seeker of donation. The king replied I am your servant, whatever you like. Uttanka said, your queen has two earrings, and my *gurupatni* wants to feed the Brahmins wearing those earrings on the occasion of Vrat. The king said you are an appropriate person to be given such donation. You go to the interior of the palace and there you demand this from my wife. The *brahmachari* Uttanka entered the interior portion of the palace. He could not see the queen in the palace. He came back to the king and was angry with him. The king thought for sometime. No man with unclean mouth can see my wife. You must have an unclean mouth. Then he remembered, that in a hurry he hadn't washed his mouth properly. So Uttanka washed his mouth properly and then went inside the palace. The queen stood at his arrival. Uttanka said that the teacher's wife wants your two earrings for Vrat and feeding the Brahmins. Then the queen was very happy but warned that these earrings are desired by nagtakshak, so be very careful on the way. Now, Takshak assumed the shape of a *sadhu* and followed Uttanka. Uttanka rested near a water place. He took a bath and in the meantime takshak picked up the two earrings and went away. Uttanka followed him. Takshak entered a hole in the earth and went to the *Naglok*. Now Uttanka started digging the hole to reach Takshak. So Indra sent Vajra to dig. Vajra entered the stick of Uttanka and dug the hole. Uttanka then entered the *Naglok* to search for the earrings taken by Takshak. There he saw a horse. He was asked to blow in the hind portion of the horse. So there was a smoke and Takshak and all the brothers were suffocating, so they came and handed over the tworings to Uttanka. Now, Uttanka was worried, he had come such a great distance from the Ashram of the *guru*. He was asked to ride the same horse. It was the fourth day and the *gurupatni* was prepared with the *Vrat*. She was angry and prepared to curse Uttanka because he didn't arrive with the earrings. He suddenly arrived on the horse and he presented the two earrings. *Gurupatni* was happy and performed the vrat and fed the Brahmins. The *guru* was also happy and blessed him that all the knowledge of Shastras will flash to him automatically.

❑

Bhrigu

Bhrigu *rishi* was a powerful person. He was the founder of the Bhargav clan of *rishis*. Chavan *rishi* was his son. Bhrigu *rishi* was married to Puloma a *rakshasa kanya* and he was living with his wife happily in his *ashram*. One day, another man named Puloma came in search of Puloma the *rishipatni*. He asked everybody if they knew Puloma. Ultimately, he asked *agni devta*. *Agni devta* said you loved Puloma but you were not married to her in my presence so she was not your legal wife. So you cannot claim her. But he wanted to take back Puloma by force. He said, Puloma had accepted him as her husband. So he has a claim over her. He went in the presence of Puloma and he wanted to take possession of Puloma by force. At this Puloma assumed the shape of a boar and ran as fast as wind and kidnapped Puloma the *rishipatni*. There was a child in the womb of Puloma. He was so angry with the behaviour of the man who was in the shape of animal trying to kidnap his mother. He dropped out of the womb of the mother. At the sight of the bright child

out of the womb of the mother, Puloma the *rakshasa* gave up the kidnapped woman and he was immediately burnt to ashes. Puloma the *rishipatni* was unconscious and she took up her son in lap and went to Brhmaji. Brahmaji saw the Puloma shedding tears. He consoled her and the river formed out the drop of her tears came to be known as Vadhusara. The river still flows near the Chavan rishi's ashram. Then Bhrigu came to see his son Chavan. He was very angry with Puloma his wife and he was also angry with Agni who had revealed the identity of Puloma the *rishipatni*. The *rishi* cursed the agni. Now, *rishi* Chavan was once in meditation in a forest. His whole body was covered with dust and his two eyes were brightly shining in the dust heap. The daughter of a king came there with her friends. She looked at the strange scene of the light coming out of heap of dust and grass. Out of curiosity she picked up a sharp twig and pierced into the bright light coming out of the dust and grass heap. Blood started coming out of the eyes. The *rishi* woke up from his meditation and he cursed the person who had pierced his eyes. Now the king and his entourage were all suffering from some gastric problem. They were all restless. The king found out the cause that his daughter was the cause of this. The king came for pardon before the *rishi*. The *rishi* prayed to God Ashwini Kumar. They came and they prepared a medicine for him. They said that after taking this the *rishi* will be youth again. So that medicine is called Chavanprash even today. The rishi'S eyes were restored and he was married to that princess who had pierced his eyes. As he had dropped in anger from the womb of his mother. He was called Chavan.

Bhim, the First Pandava to Marry

While the Pandavas were in the dark forest near the town of Ekchakra, they were very tired. So Bhim protected them and they all slept soundly on the bare ground. Bhim lamented that Kunti who was the daughter of a great king and wife of Pandu had to sleep on hard ground. Yudhishthira and other princes who deserved better luxury of life were deprived of even the bare comforts. This was because of the evil designs of Duryodhana. In the neighbourhood, there was a *rakshasa* called Hidamb and his sister Hidamba. Hidamb asked his sister to go and kill the men for their flesh since long he had been deprived of human flesh. Now that it was available he was very much glad to have the human flesh. He would imagine to burst the nerves of men and drink hot blood. Hidamba the sister, goes to the place where the Pandavas were sleeping. She assumed a human self and she became most beautiful and attractive to look at. She saw Bhim as a bright young man with robust body and youthful attraction.

She forgot the idea of killing. Kamdev had pierced her heart. She called Bhim to reciprocate the love. In the meantime, Kunti woke up and all the Pandavas woke up. Hidamba pleaded with Kunti to permit her son to marry her. She also pleaded with the eldest Pandav Yudhishthira to allow Bhim to marry her.

When there was delay in the execution, Hidamb the *rakshasa* came to the scene. He was angry with the sister about why she hadn't brought the body of the man for his food. Bhim challenged him to wrestling. Other Pandavas were sleeping and their sleep would be disturbed so Bhim took them to a distance for the fight. In the meantime, the Pandavas woke up and saw the scene of fight between Bhim and Hidamb. Arjun was very anxious to kill the *Rakshasa* Hidamb. They offered to fight together. However, Bhim said he would tackle the problem singlehanded. There was delay so Arjun said the Rakshasas gain more power in the night and soon there will be night and it will be difficult to tackle him. Thereupon Bhim took up the body and whirled it a hundred times and then threw it on the ground. The *Rakshasa* was thrown on the ground. And Bhim broke his body into two pieces and Hidamb died soon. Now his sister Hidamba proposed to Bhim to marry her but he was angry with her because she was a *Rakshasi*. Ultimately, Kunti and Yudhishthira agreed on a condition that she would take Bhim in the morning and whole day she would entertain him and by evening he should be brought to the Pandavas and when the first child is born then this marriage will be over. So it went on. She agreed on that condition. After some time a child was born, he had no hairs in his body and so he was called Ghatotkachha. Just after birth he grew fast tall and strong, and he bowed before his parents, and grandmother Kunti, and other Pandavas. He could cross valleys, hills and mountains. He had the greatest strength. This is the situation under which Bhim became the first among the Pandavas to marry and produce a child.

❑

The First Son of Kunti

Kunti was the daughter of the king. She was very beautiful to look at. Once *Rishi* Durvasa visited the king's house. He was famous for his anger, but Kunti managed the Rishi's affairs in such a way that he was forced to bestow some boon on her. One of the boons was that the with help of the recitation of the *mantras*, any god propitiated would appear before her. For a long time she forgot the power of the *mantra*. One day she was standing on her window and she saw the bright sun in the eastern sky. Curiosity led her to propitiate the Sun God with the mantra given by Durvasa. Suddenly, the sun god in his gorgeous *avtar* appeared before Kunti. She was nervous. She had just tested the *mantra* out of curiosity but low and behold the Sun God was there. The Sun God asked why Kunti had propitiated and called him. She could not reply. The Sun God said I cannot be called without purpose. He persuaded her to reciprocate his love.

And the Sun God disappeared. After sometime a child was born with *Kavach* and *Kundal*. Kunti was nervous. She did not like people to know that she had

given birth a child as a virgin. So she devised means to dispose of the child. She put some ornaments and valuables in the box and let the box flow in the river. After a long distance of the box floating in the river, a man, got the box from the flowing water. He was charioteer by profession. His wife was childless. When she saw the child, she was overwhelmed with emotion. Now the child was being nursed, educated and trained under the guidance of this family. His name was Karna. He always thought that he was their son. Ultimately, Karna came in contact with the Kaurvas. Those days, *Rishi* Parshuram was very famous and powerful. Parashuram had eliminated the Kshatriyas eighteen times on the earth and he had donated the land to Kapil. Kshatriyas were afraid of him. However, Karna reached his *ashram* for education and training of weapons. *Rishi* Parshuram thought that he was a Brahmin. One day when the *rishi* was tired he was taking rest on the thigh of Karna. A deadly insect sharply wounded the thigh of Karna but he did not flinch and did not disturb the sleep of the rishi. The flow of warm blood awakened the *rishi* from his sleep. He asked him what is your caste? You cannot be a Brahmin because a Brahmin does not have so much of tolerance. The *rishi* was angry with him and cursed him that he would forget the formula of the weapons at the time when it would be needed the most. Now, Karna came in contact with Kaurvas and particularly Duryodhan in the final tournament of games. He was not allowed to participate because he was not a king or a prince. Immediately, Duryodhan declared him the king of Magadh and he was very much obliged. He was a great dani. Every day he would take bath in the river Ganga and within the next one hour oblige anyone and everyone's request. Now Indra was in favour of his son, Arjun so he got *Kavach* and *Kundal* as *daan* from Karna. Now, during the Mahabharata war Karna was never allowed to become head of the army, because Bheeshmapitamah was not in his favour. Only after the death of Bhishma Dronacharya, he was appointed the commander of the Kaurav army. Many times Krishna and Kunti persuaded his to change sides and come with the Pandavas. However, he never agreed. He had given promise to Kunti that he will not kill anybody among the Pandavas except Arjun. He kept his promise. On the final day of judgment his chariot was stuck in the mud of blood in the battlefield. He was killed by Arjun while he was trying to lift the wheel of his chariot. He was armless.

❑

How Bhim Saved the Town Ekchakra

In the city of Ekchakra, the Pandavas took shelter in the house of a poor Brahmin. They used to move in the forest and banks of rivers and enjoyed beautiful gardens and for their livelihood they were dependent on begging for alms. People used to say that these Brahmins are not made for begging alms. Their good behaviour and their divine deportment makes them fit for kingship. The people of the town were always ready to offer alms to the Pandavas. Everyday at the evening, the brothers would bring their total amount of alms gathered to mother Kunti. The mother used to cook and half the food was served to Bhim and the other half was served to all the brothers and Kunti. The Pandavas passed many days in the town. One day, Yudhishthira and other three brothers went out for alms and Bhim was left with the mother. Suddenly, there was a great cry from the house of the Brahmin where they were living. At this Kunti could not bear the pain and she went to the Brahmin family to know about the cause of

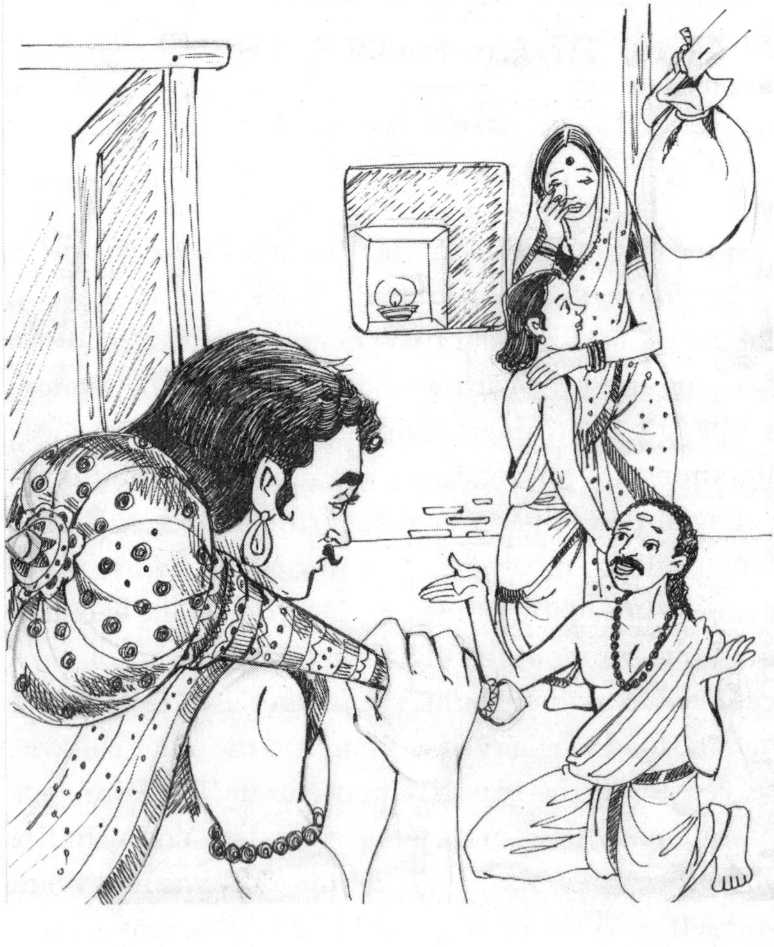

their trouble. Kunti entered into the house of the Brahmin. She overheard a discussion going on among the Brahmin, his wife, son and daughter. Brahmin was saying, I should go to the Rakshasa, my life is useless and life is full of problems. He told his wife, "This place is not worth living, there is no good king, and I always wanted you to leave this place and go to other town. You didn't agree, since your family was here. You were attached to them. Now they are all gone from the world. You arc a faithful wife to me. You have served me like a mother. You have given me a son and a daughter. Now no more work is left for me in the world. Even if I die, you will be able to maintain the two children." Then the mother replied, "I am your wife. The duty of a wife is to sacrifice herself for the husband and if I sacrifice for you I will merit heaven. I am a woman, I cannot protect my daughter. People want to exploit widows, so better if I die before you. If I die, you may have second wife." Then the son said, "a son is born to give happiness to the parent. If I die, you can produce another son. So it is better that I should face the danger." Then the daughter intervened, "A daughter is a burden, if father and mother are no more, the life of the daughter will be a hell. My brother, who is himself a child cannot protect me. So it is better, I die to save you all. My claim for death is better than any of you." Kunti was listening to all these arguments. She revealed herself to the Brahmin, and asked, "What is the problem?, Why do you talk of death? " Then the Brahmin said, at a distance of four miles from the town, there is a king, in the cave dwells Rakshasa called Bakasur. He used to attack the town and kill large number of people daily. So the town elders struck a bargain with him – 20 kilos of rice, and one man would carry the food to him and the food and the man would be eaten by Bakasur. Today is the turn of my family, to send the man with the food for Bakasur. Kunti said, you prepare the food, I have five sons, if one of my sons go for Bakasur, still four will be left. Then she confided in Brahmin and said that don't tell this to anybody. My son knows a *mantra* and he will defeat the Rakshasa. Then Kunti discussed this with Yudhishthira and said that I have decided to send Bhim to the Bakasur with food. I know Bhim is very strong. When he was a child he slipped from the rock and fell on another rock, which as a result of his impact was turned into pieces. So, ultimately, Yudhishthira agreed with the views of his mother in sending Bhim to Bakasur. As planned, Bhim collected the food, carried it on his head and went to that part of the forest, where Bakasur lived. He sat down on the ground and spread the food before him. He started eating the food himself and shouted the name of Bakasur again and again. Bakasur heard it and appeared on the scene. He was very much amazed to find this defiance. He came near Bhim, and with his hand struck on the back of Bhim, but Bhim caught hold of his hand and kept eating. Then the Rakshasa uprooted a tree and threw it at him. Bhim did not stop eating. He only kept laughing. When he had finished the food he was now ready to reciprocate the fight. He caught hold of the body of the Rakshasa and crushed him. Bakasur cried aloud, then he lifted his body and threw it on the ground. His middle portion of the body was broken and lot of blood came out of his mouth, and he was dead. Now Bhim, dragged the body to the gate of the town and stealthily he came home. So, when it was morning, people saw the dead body and recognised it to be Bakasur. So they consulted the chart who's duty it was to supply food to the Bakasur that night. So they came to the Brahmin and asked him how Bakasur died. The Brahmin replied, that there was a kind Brahmin who saved us by taking the duty on himself. Thus, it was that Bhim saved the city of Ekchakra from the strocities of Bakasur.

How Bhim Became Brikodar

Once king Duryodhan devised a plan to kill Bhim. He arranged a camp on the river bank and all the princes including Pandavas were invited to share the water sport. Large tents were raised, delicious food was arranged and all sorts of means of pleasure were provided in the camp. The water sport began. Bhim had a great appetite. He could digest large quantity of food. In childhood, Kunti used to serve half the food prepared to Bhim and half was served to other brothers. Bhim was provided enough eating and drinking in the camp by the men of Duryodhan. He was drugged with poison and somebody put him in the river. Duryodhan announced that perhaps Bhim has already left for home ahead of others. So Yudhishthira and others came to capital city Hastinapur and asked mother Kunti about whereabouts of Bhim. She did not know about Bhim. So Vidur was consulted and appraised of apprehension of Bhim being killed by the Kaurvas. Vidur advised not to reveal this to anybody.

Now, Bhim while drowned in river was bitten by *nags*/serpants. So his poison was removed. The *nags* asked their elders to recognise the man. The elders recognised him as his grandchild from mothers' side. He was very happy. The *nags* were very happy to entertain. He was given drinks out of eighth *kunds*, i.e. pits. Thus, Bhim got the strength of 10,000 elephants in the body. He was also given the *mantra* of digesting all sorts of poison. Thus, Bhim became Brikodar.

When Bhim Met Hanuman

Bhim was living at Gandhmadan hills. Beyond that was the territory of Indra. Now Arjun had gone, to learn handling of weapons from Indra. He was considered son of Lord Indra. One day, beside a river, Bhim was sitting with Draupadi. Suddenly, a bright lotus flower came before him. Bhim leapt into water and brought the lotus flower for Draupadi. Draupadi was very happy. She wanted to present the flower to King Yudhishthira, so she persuaded Bhim to bring another lotus flower. Bhim proceeded to the place of lotus flower. On the way, there was a big forest of banana. When Bhim entered the banana field he found an old man, lying across the way. He requested the old man to give way to him. The old man said I am very tired and I am taking rest. Why do you disturb me. The old man said, you may cross over my body. Bhim said every living being was a part of the divine living being. I can't cross over your body. Bhim tried to remove the tail of the old monkey with his left toe. He could not do that. He had to apply more strength but could not move the tail. Now he was surprised. He said sir, you must be some divine force. Tell me who you are. Then Hanuman revealed his identity. Bhim was greatly surprised. Bhim was supposed to be son of Lord Vayu and Hanuman was also Vayuputra. So both were brothers. Hanuman was very glad to meet Bhim. Bhim asked him to tell the story of Ram. He briefly told him the story of Ramayana. Bhim requested Hanuman to show the body he assumed at the time of crossing the sea. Hanuman showed the body to him. Hanuman could assume the smallest and the biggest of his body. He had *sidhhis*. Now, Bhim told Hanuman how Pandavas were preparing to fight the unethical and immoral government of Kauravas. So Hanuman blessed Bhim, assured him that during the battle of Mahabharata he would be on the flag of Arjun and in the roar of Bhim and it would increase many times in volume. To put fear in the enemies and the chariot of Arjun will be heavier than its weight because Hanuman would be in the flag.

❑

Dharmaraj Born as Vidur

Rishi Mandavya was a great yogi. He was standing on the gate of his ashram. There was a tree on the gate of his ashram. Under the tree, he was standing in *maunvrat,* raising two hands upwards. In this difficult *vrat,* many days passed. One day, some thieves entered the ashram with some stolen goods. They were followed by the government police. The police recovered the stolen property and some of the thieves from the ashram. When asked, the *rishi* did not speak anything, because he was under *maunvrat*. This aroused the suspicion of the officers and they produced *rishi* Mandavya to the court of the king. The king decided along with the thieves, Mandavya was to be put on Cross (*suli*) till death. The *rishi* was also put on suli. Thus, after hanging them on the *suli* the officers returned home. Maharshi Mandavya did not die on the *suli.* He did not get any food, but this didn't do him any harm. He survived and with his power of penance he called other *sadhus* and talked with them. They used to come to him in the guise of birds. The visitors in the form of birds used to ask about the sin that he had

committed, that he was forced to sit on the *suli*. Mandavya replied, "I don't blame anybody. Nobody has done me any harm."

Now the king heard of the report of the survival of Mandavya *rishi* and his activities. The king consulted his advisors and decided to please Maharshi Mandavya. The king said, "Out of ignorance I have put you on *suli*". You should not be angry with me. Tell me what I am to do to please you. Maharshi Mandavya was pleased to hear this from the king. The king ordered his removal from the *suli*. They tried to remove the *suli*, in doing so, the upper portion of the *Suli* was broken and the lower portion remained stuck in his body. Now the rishi was moving around with the half suli in his body. One day while moving around he came to the palace of Dharmaraja. He was called Animandavya. He came to the Dharmaraja's house and saw him sitting in his throne. He asked what crime has he committed for which he was given this punishment. I must know this immediately. Then you will see the power of my penance. Dharmaraja replied, you had pierced pin in the back of the innocent insects. That has resulted in this punishment, because whatever good or bad you do it will multiply many times. Rishi Animandavya said that tell me at what age did I commit this sin? Dharmraja replied, in childhood you had done this sin. Animandavya said, according to law of the *Dharma*, a child till the age of twelve is not considered fit for punishment of the crime. You have punished me disproportionately. Killing of a Brahmin is a supreme crime. You will be born in a Shudra caste as a man. I announce from today the limitation of law that till the age of fourteen years nobody will be punished for his crime. Only person above fourteen year can be liable for punishment of his sin. That is why the curse of Mandavya forced Dharmaraja to be born as Vidur in Shudra class. That is why Vidur was great scholar of Dharmashastra and arthshastra. He was free from worldly desires. He had forseeability and he was always interested in the good of the Kaurvas and Pandavas as a minister.

❑

Akshaypatra of Yudhishthira

Once King Yudhishthira with his priests and servants was camping in a forest. He was very much worried, how to feed the large number of visitors and dependents. So, when a *rishi* called on him, he asked for a solution. The *rishi* said you go to the Ganga and take bath in the river and stand in the water, and recite some *mantra* to please the sun God. The Sun God Would tell the solution. Yudhisthira went to the river Ganga and stood in the water and recited the *mantra* as told by the rishi. Then Sun God was pleased and he asked him to ask for a boon. Yudhishthira said, Lord, I have to feed lot of dependents in this forest and I cannot maintain them properly, so kindly find a solution. The Sun God offered him a small utensil and said as long as Draupadi, the queen does not take food out of it, it can serve as many people as you like. So, he was happy with the utensil and came and offered it to queen Draupadi. The king directed the queen to serve the food from that utensil to all the people who needed food.

One day, *rishi* Durvasa came with his entourage of *sadhus* and *sanyasis*. He was persuaded by Duryodhana

to pay a visit and enjoy the hospitality of King Yudhishthira. The *rishi* Durvasa reached with his group and demanded food at odd hours. Draupadi had already taken food and cleaned the pot. So they said sir you take bath, and in the meanwhile we will prepare food for you. Durvasa went there for bath. In the meantime, Draupadi found that her pot was empty, so she prayed to Lord Krishna. She knew that Durvasa would curse her, if he was not given food. So Lord Krishna appeared on the scene and asked her, to see if there is anything in your pot. Draupadi said there was nothing. Lord Krishna insisted Draupadi to search again and she found a small blade of grass in the pot. Lord Krishna took it and ate it himself. Durvasa and his entourage were bathing in the river, suddenly they felt that their belly was full and that they could not take any food, and they all ran away from the scene. Thus, the plan of Duryodhana to manage curse from Durvasa to King Yudhishthira was unsuccessful.

❑

Invention of Umbrella

Jamdagni was a famous *rishi*. His son was Parashuram. He was called so, because he always kept a *parshu* a weapon with his. He was also considered the incarnation of Lord Vishnu. Now, Jamdagni had three sons. One day, the king of Mahishmati, raided the ashram of Jamdagni. They humiliated his wife Renuka. Renuka was very beautiful to look at. Rishi Jamdagni was angry with Renuka for her contact with Mahishmati. So he ordered his sons to behead Renuka. Two sons did not agree. Parashuram immediately followed the orders of his father and beheaded his mother. Rishi Jamdagni blessed his son.

At the plea of the son, the life of mother, i.e. Renuka was revived. One day Jamdagni was practising arrow shooting. It was a hot sunny day, the Rishi would shoot the arrow to great distance. Renuka used to pick up the arrow and bring to the Rishi again. In so doing she said My Lord, in this hot sun I am sweating profusely. Please

kindly devise some means to give me relief. The rishi, invented a device to protect his wife from sun and heat. Thus, he was the first inventor of Umbrella which protects people from sun, heat and rains.

❑

How the Pandavas were Saved in Varnavat

King Duryodhana was always scheming to damage the life and image of the Pandavas. The Pandava and Kaurva youths had already completed their education and training under the guidance of Dronacharya. Now they were to take practical lessons in the administration of the State. By show Duryodhana schemed through his supporters and friends to persuade Dhritarashtra to send the Pandavas to the city of Varnavat. There was going to be a festival for worshipping Lord Shiv. So one day, Dhritarashtra called Yudhishthira and asked him to go to Varnavat to mix with the people on the occasion of Shiv worship. Vidur understood the scheme and he kept tap on the movement of Duryodhana and his parents. When Dhritarashtra ordered Yudhishthira to go to Varnavat, people at large knew his motive of malicious designs. The people wanted to go with Pandavas but Yudhishthira persuaded them to stay at home in his best interest. Purochan was a confidant of Duryodhana.

Duryodhana called Purochan and confided in him the scheme. He said you are my second self. You will keep it to yourself. You should go to Varnavat immediately and build a house there with inflammable materials like oil, *ghee* and bamboo and other such incendiary materials. The house should be plastered with such materials. Nobody should know the scheme of inflammable materials being used in the building. So Purochan proceeded post-haste to Varnavat. And he engaged his servants and workers to complete the job. The house named Shivamangal was raised on the outskirts of the town. Purochan himself guarded the house. Now on a certain date the Pandavas with their mother Kunti arrived in the city. The people of the city organised big welcome for the Pandavas on the gate of the city. They knew that the Pandavas were the sons of their beloved ex-king Pandu who looked after the people as their father. Pandavas greeted everybody and every class of people. Ultimately, Purochan took them to lodge in the house which was meant for them. Vidur had spoken to Yudhishthira in code language that he was going to a place of danger. There was every chance of his being burnt alive. So he should devise ways to escape the tragedy. Yudhishthira called Bhim and told him he smelt foul. The house was smelling as if it was constructed of incendiary material. So the Pandavas did not protest. They took the abode in a normal way. Now Vidur sent a tunnel digger and he met Yudhishthira. Yudhishthira knew him and appreciated his effort to save the Pandavas. Then the Pandavas everyday used to go out to forest for hunting. They made themselves familiar with the area. Now the tunnel digger started his work and he did not dig from the house. Nobody could guess that there was a tunnel being dug, not even Purochan. On the night decided by Purochan to inflame the house a group of a Brahmin family with five sons and mother came to stay in the house. Men of Purochan set fire to the house, at appointed time and the Pandavas escaped through the tunnel, the five sons of the Brahman along with their mother were burnt alive and people mistook them for Pandavs and mother Kunti. Pardovas knew the area thoroughly, so they escaped and the boatman carried them beyond river. Thus, the town people saw the house where the Pandavas were lodged burning. They were sad. They said the Kaurvas had done the mischief to eliminate the Pandavas. Yudhishthira decided to remain incognito. Kunti and her sons disguised themselves because they apprehended that Duryodhana would find out and kill them. When the news of burning of the house reached Hastinapur, King Dhritarashtra paid last rites and distributed food to the Brahmins as *Shradha* ceremony. People at large knew that the Kaurvas were mischief mongers and they have killed the Pandavas and mother Kunti in the fire.

❑

Fisherman Daughter became the Queen

A fisherman's daughter was ferrying passengers across the Jamuna river. One day Rishi Parashar came to their place. He had to cross the river by boat. The boat was ferried by fisherman's daughter Satyavati. Rishi Parashar boarded the boat. He was alone in the boat. So in the middle of the river rishi was overwhelmed with passion for the girl. The girl pointed out that there were people on both sides of the river. Rishi created mist by power of Yoga and he fulfilled his desire with the girl. Now the girl was given two boons. One, she would always remain virgin and second that the aroma of her body would spread for one *yojan*. She was now called Yojangandha. Rishi Parashar giving these two boons he went away.

Those days King Shantanu was ruling over Hastinapur. He had his son, Devabrat. It so happened that the king went on a hunting mission with his officers

and soldiers. He visited that portion of the island which was the abode of Satyavati Yojangandha. Now this fisherman's daughter had a son called Vyas, from Parashar who compiled the Vedas. The king happened to see the girl and he was very much fascinated. He wanted to marry her, but he knew that he had a son Devabrat and he should not marry. The king returned to the capital city of Hastinapur. He was very sad in love of the fishergirl. He gave up food and drink and all sorts of entertainments. He did not take interest in the affairs of the state. This became the talk of the town. Now Devabrat came to know about it. He immediately left for the island and he met the father of the girl Satyavati. The father said, he had one condition that if the king married my daughter, her first child will be the king after Shantanu. Devabrat said I am the first son of the king. I declare that I will abjure my claim in favour of the child born out of Shantanu and Satyavati. Then he said, no, suppose you don't claim but your children may claim the throne of Hastinapur, then Devabrat declared that whosoever living or non-living should listen to my promise that I will never marry and remain *Brahmachari*. So this was a very difficult promise and people said that this is *Bheeshan* promise so Devabrat was called Bheeshma after that and this name stuck to him ever since. Now the fishergirl was brought to Hastinapur and married to King Shantanu. Thus, a fisherman's daughter became the queen of Hastinapur and the *kuruvansh* subsequent kings became the descendants of Satyavati, the fishergirl.

❑

The Birth of Draupadi and her Brother

The Panchals were a powerful force. The king of Panchals Raja Drupad was against the immoral and illegal ways in which the Kaurvas were treating the Pandavas. King Drupad was a classmate of Dronacharya. Dronacharya was a Brahmin, but he had mastered the art of weapon welding and instructing the ward of kings. Dronacharya was the teacher of Kaurvas and Pandavas and he also accepted Dhrishtadumna, the son of King Drupad as his student. During the student days in the ashram, King Drupad and Dronacharya were great friends. After coming out from the ashram, Dronacharya was in a poor condition. He had no means to sustain his family. His son was given rice water instead of milk. Wife of Dronacharya requested him to go to his old friend King Drupad. He took a journey to capital of Panchal. The King Drupad did not pay much respect to him. Dronacharya was very much surprised. When he came in the presence of the King Drupad, he felt humiliated. The

king offered him only the customary alms given to Brahmins. Dronacharya felt very bad. He told the king about his feelings. The king replied that after all he was a Brahmin and now Drupad was a king. So now he could not be treated as he was treated in the ashram days. So, Dronacharya returned humiliated. King Drupad had no son, no daughter. He took the help of a vedic Brahmin called Vaaj. He persuaded the scholar to perform a *yajna* for him so that he gets a son and a daughter for him. *Yajna* started in seriousness. When Vaaj asked the queen to perform the final rite the queen was not ready as she had a *paan* in her mouth. The priest decided that the *havankund* would produce the children. So he finally decided to produce the children from the *havankund* itself. One daughter appeared. She had big eyes and she was dark in colour and attractive scent spread from her body. She was the most beautiful woman of the time. The son was called Dhrishtadumna. He was born with armour and other weapons on his body. He took a full man figure just after his birth and he rode the horse to march the army. The Panchals were very happy. King Drupad believed that Dhrishtadumna would kill Dronacharya who had dishonoured him. Thus, ultimately the marriage of Draupadi faced the king. It was decided to hold the *swayamvar*. The king believed that Draupadi should be married to Arjun. So it was announced that on certain date, a *swayamvar* will be arranged for the marriage of Draupadi. This message reached the ears of the

Pandavas, who were in hiding after the accident of Lakshagriha. They also came to the *swayamvar* and stayed in the house of a pot-maker. On the day of *Swayamwar*, a fish was hung on a tall pole and it was declared that whosoever would hit the target, i.e. the moving fish on the top of the pole, would be the winner of the hand of Draupadi. The Kaurvas also came to the *swayamwar*. Arjun hit the target and garland of acceptance was put on his neck by Draupadi. Draupadi was taken to the house of the pot-maker where the Pandavas were residing. The king wanted to find out which caste they belong to. So after some days he arranged a feast at his palace and the interest of the Pandavas in the weapons in the arms and royal emblems assured the king that they were Kshatriyas. Draupadi, although she had garlanded Arjun, she was asked by Kunti to be shared by all the Pandav brothers. This was an odd thing. The king and his royal family were upset but ultimately, Rishi Vyas convinced the king and the royal family that there was nothing wrong about it. He cited examples from history. Thus, Draupadi became the first lady empress of India. Thus, the *yajna* of Drupad produced the queen empress of India and the death warrant of Dronacharya.

❑

FABLES FROM THE MAHABHARATA

The Jackal and the Lions

In very ancient times, in a very prosperous city named Purika, there was a famous king called Purika. He was a very mean and a cruel ruler, who used to torture innocent creatures. His old age was full of miseries. So after his death, he was reborn as a jackal.

The king reborn as a jackal could remember the prosperity and luxury of his previous birth when he had been a king. He decided to lead a better life and gave up the life of indulgence. He became a hermit. He gave up meat and flesh food as well. He followed his vows and penance very religiously.

The jackal used to live in a secluded place, which was a graveyard. He was Infact born there. His ascetic way of living was not liked by his relatives and friends. They requested him again and again to accept the ways of a common jackal. They told him to eat meat and flesh, hunt game and kill other animals, but the jackal was adamant. So his family and friends were very angry with him. The jackal often used to argue with them in a soft tone and with sweet words. He believed that a person could not achieve merit because of wealth, dynasty or status. Merit could only be achieved by personal code of conduct based on moral and ethical principles.

The news of the jackal's pious living and sincerity of speech and conduct spread far and wide. The king of the forest, a brave lion came to know the wonderful qualities of his head and heart. He went to the jackal and paid high respects to him. He requested him to accept the post of a minister in his cabinet. The lion said, "Dear friend, I am aware of your great qualities. Come along with me, and enjoy whatever you like. You are free to reject the things, which you do not like. But you must be careful in one thing. My relatives, as you know are very cruel by nature. You will have to deal with them carefully and look after our overall welfare."

The jackal greatly appreciated the polite words of the lord of the forest. He bowed his head and pleaded in sweet words, "Sir, it is quite befitting your status that you are in search of an honest, hard working and sincere assistant to run your affairs. Without ministers and advisors, a ruler cannot manage his country well. He cannot rule over a vast empire by himself. He must therefore select faithful, knowledgeable, liberal persons, deft at diplomatic and political deliberations. But Sir, I am not interested in enjoying the comforts of a royal palace. I am happy with my frugal living. Your old advisors and servants may not like my nature and behaviour. Most of them are rogues. They may keep speaking against me to you, in private. Sir, you are brave, kind-hearted, and fortunate. I am a free person, and I do not know the ways and etiquette of the royal palace.

Often kings have punished more innocent people than the real culprits because of court conspiracies.

Yet, if you insist on appointing me as your minister, I have a few conditions, and you will kindly deal with me accordingly. You will kindly pay respect to my relatives. You must listen to my advice in your interest. Whatever is my salary etc. you will kindly keep it with yourself. I will not sit in committees with other ministers. I will advise you in private. Your ministers may be jealous of me. You will never ask my advice on how to deal with your relatives. If on my advice, you find out the mistakes committed by your other advisors, do not award capital punishment to them. You will never attack my relatives even if you are angry."

The lion accepted the conditions of the wise jackal. So the jackal was duly appointed as the chief councilor of the ruler. His counsels were highly beneficial to the lion. Very soon the jackal began commanding high respect.

Old ministers and councilors grew jealous of the jackal. Some of them grew so hostile that they formed a group against the jackal. They tried to poison his mind and tried hard to make him as corrupt as they themselves were. They were selfish, always on the look out to usurp others' wealth or property. Now they could not do so. The jackal had put a stop to all this.

He had promulgated strict rules against, corrupt practices of the government officers. So the old ministers and officers always tried to please and persuade the jackal to follow their corrupt ways. Soon they realized that it was of no use trying to corrupt the jackal. Finally the disgruntled officers of the lion decided to teach the jackal a lesson.

One day, these corrupt officers hid the royal meat and flesh specially prepared for the lord of the jungle, the lion, in the residential quarters of the jackal. The jackal knew about the plan and the person who executed the conspiracy, but he kept the secret to himself.

When the lion was hungry and came to the dining table, he did not find the meat that had been specially prepared for him.

The lion ordered his servants to find the thief. After some time one of the servants, who had in fact planned the conspiracy, informed the lion that the special food was hidden in the residence of the jackal. Some of the old servants said that the jackal was a hypocrite.

The lion was in great anger at the behaviour of the jackal. He decided to kill him. Now the old advisors found an opportunity to fan this flame of anger. They said, "Sir, he can do all sorts of heinous crimes. Our Lord had thought very highly of him. But he is a mean fellow. How dare he betray His Excellency, the ruler of this forest! His religious and morally high words were just a show. In fact he is a clever cheat."

The lion's servant showed the food with the jackal. Now the lion was sure that the jackal was the culprit. He ordered the jackal to be executed without delay. This news spread like wild fire in the jungle.

The lion's mother heard and came to the lion's court. She said, "Dear son, I smell a conspiracy. It is not wise to take hasty decisions. In royal courts, people are jealous of one another. Even hermits, saints, and sages have friends and enemies. A greedy person is jealous of a liberal one, a coward does not like a brave one and a poor person is hostile to the rich. So also a fool is jealous of a wise scholar, and an ugly person will speak ill of a handsome and charming personality. Even among great scholars some are greedy and jealous of others. They keep searching for defects in great scholars.

Your food had been stolen from an unguarded kitchen. Here is this jackal that does not accept flesh as food even if offered with respect. Remember my son, some people look decent but in fact they are rogues. Others look rough but they may be kind at heart. All that glitters is not gold. The sky looks like a convex utensil, but it is not so in reality. The fireflies glow in the darkness, but there is no fire in them. So, one must examine things with care. The apparent is not always the real.

Dear son, you appointed the jackal as your chief councilor. He acquired name and fame because of his merit and honesty. It is rare to find people like him. He is loyal to you. A king should not punish an innocent person."

Very soon some other confidential secret agents informed the king about the real culprit. The lion pardoned the wise jackal. The lion also expressed regret for the baseless charges he had levied against the honest jackal.

The jackal went on a fast and thought of ending his life. But the lion entreated and dissuaded him from that course of action.

Now the jackal said, "Sir you brought me here with great honour and gave me proper respect. But due to the conspirators I feel humiliated. My life was threatened. Now I do not feel that I am fit to serve you. A ruler should always remain cautious of a person whom he has humiliated. Such people wait for the opportunity to harm the ruler. It is easier for the enemy to enlist disgruntled servants to harm the ruler. Once I have lost your confidence, it is also not possible for me to have full faith in you. Your old servants may again conspire against me, hence it is not safe for me to stay here any more. Once broken, the line of love, confidence and loyalty cannot be fully restored."

The wise jackal did not accept the renewed offer of the lion. He left the palace, and spent the rest of his life in penance as a hermit in his own native place.

❑

Rajdharma and Brahmin Gautam

Long, long ago, in a northern country, there was a dense forest. A famous bandit king used to live there. But he was very kind to poor and needy persons. One day a poor Brahmin named Gautam came to his place. He had no knowledge of the scriptures. His ancestors were famous scholars. But there were hardly any characteristics of a Brahmin in him. Yet the bandit king welcomed him. He made necessary arrangement for his residence and appointed a woman to look after his household.

The poor Brahmin, Gautam began living in the village of the bandit king. He also went hunting with bows and arrows. He killed animals, and gradually he became just like any other inmate of the forest. His hair grew wild, his body turned dark and dirty and he turned into a cruel hunter.

One day, by chance he learned that a mendicant had come to the bandit's village. He was very hungry and tired. He was searching for the house of a brahmin.

When he found the house of Gautam, he said, "Gautam! Your forefathers were great scholars and honorable people. They were kind and helpful to others. But what have you done to yourself?

Gautam did not speak much. He offered food and drink, but the guest did not touch them and spent the night there in great distress.

Next morning, the guest left Gautam's house. Gautam was also very sad when he thought of his degraded condition. He also left the bandit's village. He saw a group of traders going toward a port city. He joined their caravan. One night some wild elephants attacked the caravan and Gautam was separated from them. He travelled alone for many days and came to a lovely place.

There was a big banyan tree. Different variety of strange birds were chirping and singing on it. The tree looked like a big shady umbrella. Sweet breeze was blowing. Gautam sat under the tree and was soon in a deep slumber.

The sun went down and the evening spread its thin glow. Gautam looked up, and saw a bright big crane in the tree. He was the king of the cranes. His name was Rajdharma. He was decorated with glazing ornaments. Every limb of the bird was beautiful and divine.

Gautam was amazed to see such a beautiful bird. Gautam was thirsty and hungry. The long journey had made him tired. He looked at Rajdharma with greedy eyes and decided to kill him for food.

Just then the king of cranes said, "O Sir, you are welcome, this tree is my house. It is my great fortune that you have come here. Now the sun has gone down and evening has prevailed. You are an honorable guest. I intend to extend a warm welcome to you and entertain you. Tomorrow morning, you may resume your journey."

Gautam was surprised to hear the words of the bird. The crane narrated his family lineage. "I am the son of Saint Kashyap, and my mother is the daughter of Prajapti Daksha. You must accept my hospitality."

The crane prepared a soft bed of flowers under the tree. Big and small fish were available in a big river at a distance. The crane flew and came back with some fish. He collected dry leaves and picked up a sparkle from a nearby smithy to light the fire.

Gautam enjoyed the feast. Then he revealed his name to the host but did not tell him the details. Rajdharma asked Gautam the purpose of his journey. Gautam said, "O bird, I am a poor person. I am going towards the sea to earn some wealth."

The bird replied, "O Brahmin, you need not go far now. Your work will be done here itself. People get riches by four means-by inheritance, good fortune, hard work or with the help of friends."

Next morning, when Gautam was ready for the journey, Rajdharma, the crane said, "Go on this path. This will lead you to a city. It is a few kilometres from here. There the mighty King Virupaksha rules over the people. He is my close friend. On my recommendation he will give you enough wealth to satisfy your needs. Do not doubt it."

Gautam set out on the journey walking through a charming and scented forest path. He reached the city named Merubraja. It was surrounded by high mountain walls. The main gate was strong and wide and it was protected by armed guards and mechanical devices.

The great King Virupaksha had already been informed about the arrival of the poor Gautam sent by his friend Rajdharma. The king ordered his servants to produce the person before him without delay. The messengers conveyed to Gautam, that the king was very eager to see him. The poor Brahmin forgot his troubles and happily accompanied the royal servants.

Inside the palace Gautam was astonished to see the wealth and decoration. He was brought before the king. The king asked him about his family, education and his native place. From Gautam's words, the king concluded that he was brahmin only by birth. He did not deserve much. However, he was sent by his dear friend Rajdharma, so the king decided to honor him and help him.

Next day, there was a big festival in the palace. A large number of brahmins were invited, fed and given immense silver, gold and ornaments in charity.

The king told the brahmin, "You may take away as much wealth as you can. The Rakshasas, the demons have agreed not to rob you today. However, if you are found even tomorrow in this kingdom, they will not spare you."

Gautam was a greedy person. Along with other brahmins he also collected a heavy load of silver, gold, utensils and costly things. But he could not run fast due to the heavy load. Somehow, by evening he again reached the Banyan tree which was the abode of the crane.

Rajdharma the crane was happy to meet him. He extended a warm welcome, arranged for food and rest for him. Now Gautam thought of his journey ahead. It was to take many days. What would he eat on the way that was his problem? An idea came to him. The crane that stood before him was a big one. It was full of flesh. If he killed the crane, its meat would suffice for many days.

This thought comforted Gautam. The crane had immense faith in him, he did not suspect Gautam of foul play. When he was sleeping, gautam struck him with a burning log. He removed his feathers and roasted him on the burning fire. He was glad. He would not have to bother for food for many days. Now he gathered his wealth and the meat and quickly set out for his destination.

Next day, Rajdharma could not go to his friend king Virupaksha's court. The king was worried to find that his friend had been missing for two days. This was unprecedented. The king asked his son to find out the cause. The king suspected Gautam. The prince and soldiers quickly visited the big banyan tree, the abode of Rajdharma, the crane. They found his feathers scattered under the tree. The king's soldiers ran after Gautam and captured him. They also found the roasted flesh of Rajdharma in his possession.

Gautam was produced before the king. The king ordered his immediate death. He also ordered his flesh to be given to the Rakshasas. But even the Rakshasas refused to accept the flesh of such an ungrateful person as Gautam.

❑

The Mouse and the Cat

In a certain forest, there was a big banyan tree. It was covered with dense creepers and a strong net of offshoots. Various types of birds had their nests in the tree. The banyan tree was also the abode of many reptiles and wild creatures.

At the root of the tree, there lived a wise mouse in a hole that had hundreds of gates. The name of the mouse was Palita. On the tree above lived a bushy cat. His name was Lomash. The bushy cat made a meal on the variety of birds that lived on the tree.

One day a hunter spread his net on the ground. This was his usual practice at sunset. He would come back the next morning to collect his catch. It just so happened that Lomash, the cat came down the tree in search of prey. And by bad luck he was entangled in the hunter's net. The mouse Palita saw the plight of his natural enemy. He boldly ventured out to enjoy the small pieces of meat spread on the net by the hunter.

The mouse started enjoying the feast while smiling at the miserable cat. Suddenly he saw another enemy, the mongoose coming out of his abode. When the mouse looked up he saw a big owl on the tree also staring down at him with burning eyes. The name of this owl was Chandarak. He lived in a hole in the tree. The mouse found himself caught between two dangerous enemies.

He was very much afraid. While wondering what to do, an idea flashed to him. He thought, "When a person is in great distress, he should try his best to save his life by whatever means possible. At present I am in great trouble as my life is in danger. If I come to the ground the mongoose will devour me. If I stay here on the net the owl may pick me up. If I cut the net the cat will make a feast of me. But even in such a difficult situation I must remain cool. Only in this lies wisdom. The cat is my natural enemy but at present he is himself in great danger. Let me see whether this foolish cat listens to my advice. I shall make a fair offer to him. It's just possible that being in trouble he may accept my friendship. The great scholars have said that in times of trouble even a strong person should make his enemy, a friend. A wise enemy is better than a foolish friend. Now I can save my life only with the help of my enemy, the cat."

The wise mouse faced the cat from a distance and said, "Dear brother cat Lomash! Are you alive or dead? At present I am talking to you as a friend. I want to save your life. Dear brother don't be afraid, I will save you, but only if you promise not to kill me too. I have thought over the plan by which you can be free. Look!

the mongoose and the owl are in wait for me. I am afraid of that owl gazing down from the tree. You are a wise cat. Now aren't you my friend? We have lived together near this tree for a long time. O wise cat, I can free you from this net by cutting its cords with my sharp teeth, provided you don't kill me. A person may cross a river with the help of a log and with him the log also reaches the other side. So can I, help you cross this danger provided you save me from my calamity too.

The cat listened to the mouse attentively and considered his own difficult situation. He looked toward the mouse and started saying softly, "O Friend! you want to see me living. This makes me very happy. Surely I am in great trouble but you are in greater danger. We must agree on a treaty without delay. I promise to help you if you help me escape this net. I have no pride. I am at your mercy. I will do, as you want me to do. Both of us are in grave danger."

When Lomash, the cat said this, Palita the mouse, spoke further, "At present I am afraid of the mongoose so I want to hide under your belly. You must promise to protect me. Don't kill me. On the other hand that rogue, the owl is waiting to eat me up. You have to save me from him also, then I will cut the net to pieces. I take an oath that I will keep my word."

Having heard this proposal from the mouse, Lomash the cat looked at him as his saviour. He extended a warm welcome to him "May God bless you. Come here quickly to me. You are as dear to me as my own life. My life can be saved now only because of your kindness. So my friend, come and let us strike an alliance. Brother, after this danger is over, I will engage my friends and relations to protect your interest." The mouse replied, "Brother after this danger is over I will also serve your interest well."

The mouse was confident that the cat realising his own interest, would protect him. So he happily went to the cat and sat comfortably in his lap. The cat also made him fearless and the mouse slept under his belly as a child sleeps in the lap of its mother.

When the mongoose and the owl saw the mouse hiding under the cat, they were disappointed. They were also surprised to witness the newfound love between them. Ultimately they lost hope and went back to their home.

Seeing that the danger was over, the mouse came out and began slowly cutting in the net at the same time he was waiting for the hunter.

The cat was tired of the pressure of the net. He wanted freedom quickly. But he found the mouse working very slowly. So he said, "Dear Brother! Why do you work so slowly? Please hurry up. The hunter might be coming now and you should deliver me from the bondage before he arrives."

Palita, the mouse said, "Dear Brother, don't be impatient. I have proper understanding of time and I will not miss the opportunity. If a work is done before its appropriate time it may go against the interest of the doer. If I deliver you before the right time I may face danger from you. When I will see the hunter coming here with his weapon, you will be afraid of him. I will quickly finish the last knot. And that moment you will quickly climb up the tree and I will dive into my hole."

When the cat heard these words, he said, "A good person performs the work of his friends with love. Not as you do. I extended quick protection, when I found you in danger. Similarly you should also complete my work quickly. If ever in the past I have done anything against you unknowingly, kindly forget it. I surrender to you. Clean your heart of whatever ill feelings you may hold against me."

The mouse was a wise diplomat and he replied to the cat, "If one has possibility of harm from a friend, his work would be done as carefully as a snake charmer plays with a poisonous snake.

If a person has struck an alliance with a stronger person, he must be careful. He should keep the work of such a person unfinished. When the hunter will come here and you will only run for your life and not think of catching me, I will have cut up most of the knots. Now only a few knots are left. I will continue to cut them so do not get impatient."

Gradually the night passed, and Lomash feared the arrival of the hunter in the morning. At daybreak the hunter appeared with his weapon in hand. He looked like a messenger of death. The cat got nervous at his very sight. When the mouse found him quivering with fear, he quickly cut the last knot.

The cat ran away and climbed the tree to save his life. The mouse was also free from danger, and he fearlessly went back into his hole. The hunter examined his net and was disappointed to find it empty. So he too left the scene.

After sometime Lomash, the cat sitting on the branch of the tree in safety, addressed the mouse hiding in its hole. "O Brother, how is it that you buried yourself quickly into the hole, you did not even talk to me. I am very grateful to you. You have done me great service. Do not have any doubts about me. You reposed confidence in me, in time of danger and protected my life in return. You did to the best of your capacity, Now we are friends and we should both enjoy this friendship. I will ask all my friends and relatives to honor you. You are the lord of my body and my house and whatever property I have, I will surrender to you. You will be its sole manager. You are a very wise person. Kindly accept the post of my advisor and guide me as a father. I assure you on oath that I will not harm you. Do not be afraid of me."

When the mouse heard these flattering warm and soft words of the cat, he diplomatically replied, "Dear Brother, friendship is not a permanent thing, neither is enmity. It is dependent on self-interest. Sometimes friends become enemies and enemies become friends. So, one should not rely too much on a friend. In this world everybody wants safety and security. Self-interest is the sole substance on this earth. All living beings are tied to each other because of their self-interest. Now your work is over. My purpose is also served. We are natural enemies. Now you have no other purpose with me but to make me your food. We do not possess equal strength. So, there can be no agreement between us."

When the cat heard these harsh words of the mouse he said, "O Brother I assure you on oath, no sin is greater than betraying a friend. You have saved my life I also know the virtue of friendship and gratitude. You should not doubt my sincerity."

As the cat seriously praised the mouse, the latter replied, "You are a great saint to say so. Whatever I have heard from you is correct. I am happy, but I cannot have faith in you. We were friends because both of us were in danger. You are stronger than I. I am your natural food. So sir, I must be careful and protect myself from you. You should also protect yourself from your natural enemies like the hunter."

When the cat heard the name of the hunter, he left the place and went to a safer place. The mouse enjoyed resting in his hole below the tree.

❑

The Sage and the Dog

In a certain dense forest, there lived a great sage. He was forever engaged in severe penance. Hence his body was very thin and he looked physically weak. But due to long and arduous practice of yoga, he had also achieved miraculous powers. He could understand the language of birds and beasts.

A large number of forest dwellers, wild beasts, large elephants, man eating tigers, ferocious leopards, jackals and dogs used to visit this sage's cottage. They inquired of his welfare and never harmed him. In his presence, these wild beasts forgot their ferocious nature and behaved like docile domestic animals.

A small dog also lived in that area of the vast forest. He was also a regular visitor to the cottage of the sage. He gave up eating flesh, stopped killing other animals, and began to live as a vegetarian. He also began to practice yogic rites. He became a great devotee of the sage. The sage used to look after the dog's welfare and needs.

One day a strange leopard came near the sage's cottage. He was from some other place. He was hungry and thirsty. His fangs were large. He spotted the dog and wanted to attack it and make it his food.

The poor dog ran for his life to the sage. He prayed to the hermit and requested him to protect him from the leopard. The hermit recited some mantras and lo and behold! the dog was changed into a bigger leopard than the one that stood before it. The stranger leopard ran away on seeing the new leopard.

Now the dog-turned leopard was very happy. He forgot his saintly habits. He began to prey on other animals. He gave up eating the vegetarian food offered by the hermit.

After sometime, a tiger visited the hermitage. He was new to the area. He smelled the presence of the leopard and was very angry. The dog-turned leopard realised the danger.

He ran for his life to the hermit again and described the new threat to his existence. The kind hermit again recited some mantras and changed the leopard into a big and strong elephant, with sharp and pointed tusks. The stranger tiger realised the danger and quickly left the hermit's cottage compound.

Now the dog turned elephant began ruling over the forest. He began felling trees and crushing the tender creepers. He started to play in the cool water of the forest lake and destroyed the lotus plants and flowers. He was very proud of his new power.

One day a big lion appeared near the sage's cottage. It had golden hair on its neck and his roar vibrated through the forest like the thunder of clashing clouds.

The elephant was bewildered and it again ran to the hermit for safety. The hermit understood the elephant's fear. He uttered some mantras once again and changed the elephant into a strange animal, called Sharabh.

A Sharabh has eight legs and its eyes are strangely set on its head. Now the dog turned Sharabh made the lion run for its life. The lion left the forest forever.

Soon the Sharabh was the unchallenged ruler of the forest. A Sharabh has to live on the blood of beasts and animals. So, all the wild beasts of the forest were afraid of him. They began to leave that area to seek safer homes. Soon Sharabh was the undisputed master of all he surveyed.

One day a thought came to his mind. "The great sage has the power of performing miracles. He can change even insects and small animals into the most powerful and ferocious animals. If I sucked the blood of this hermit and kill him there will be no more danger to my position."

The moment this idea flashed within him, the great hermit with his yogic powers also understood the ungrateful nature of the dog. He quickly recited some powerful mantras and reduced the dangerous Sharabh into a small and weak dog again.

❑

The Vulture and the Jackal

Long ago, in Naimisharyan there lived a Brahmin. In his old age he was blessed with a son. But the child, unforunately died very young. He was the last hope of his family. So his parents and relatives wept bitterly. But they had to take him to the cremation ground for last rites. The father carried the dead child to the ground. At the ground because of fatherly love he was not being able to place the child on the ground and return home. He was hesitant. So were the relatives.

Their weeping and crying attracted the attention of a vulture. The bird reached there and he started addressing them. "Look here now that your only son is dead, there is no point in lamenting for him. Leave the body here and go home. Thousands of men and women have been brought to this ground and their friends and relatives have left them here."

The vulture said, "This place is full of ferocious animals. There are hundreds of carcasses, scattered here. This place is dreadful. There is no hope of this dead child coming back to life again, so leave him here and go home as soon as you can. Everyone born on this earth has to depart from the material world sooner or later. Look! the sun is on the verge of sinking. Soon it will be very dark so it is better for you to go along your way quickly."

When the Brahmin and the relatives heard the philosophical words of the Vulture, they cried even more loudly. They put the dead body of the young child on the ground and prepared to leave the place.

Suddenly there appeared a black jackal before them. The jackal started to address them, "You human beings, you people are very cruel. O fools, it is not night yet, don't be afraid. Express your love for the child! Sometimes even dead people come back to life. May be in some auspicious moment, this child may revive. How can you be so cruel to throw him away on this hard ground? It seems to me that you never loved this child. This is the child whose sweet words used to thrill your heart. Even birds and beasts, love their children better than human beings. They do not get any benefit from their progeny. Even then, they protect their children. You people are heartless. You should weep for your beloved child for a longer pereod."

The jackal continued, "Look, at his face, look at his lovely limbs. How lovely are his lotus-like eyes? His body is well washed and garlanded. How can you leave such an angel and go home?"

Having heard these sorrowful words of the jackal the relatives returned to where they had left the dead body.

Now the vulture was surprised. He started his lecture, "Oh! You foolish people are being misguided by the foolish and cruel-hearted Jackal. The body of this child is now as cold as a wooden log. All his sense organs are defunct. Why do you lament his death? One day you will also have to face this. Begin penance so that your sins are also washed. The fate of man is borne along with his body. Whatever wealth - gold, silver or jewels, sons or daughters, one gets, are because of penance."

The vulture continued, "The individual is born with a good or evil life according to his own acts of the previous birth. A father's actions will not have any bearing on his son, neither the son's on the father. Man has to tread his lonely path, himself, Leave aside attachment for this child. Leave him alone and go home. Death is all-powerful. Death does not spare anyone. Wise or fool, rich or poor, great or small, all are equal in his court. He does not spare a child, or a youth, or the aged. He can enter even the womb of a mother to kill the child. This is the reality of the world."

The jackal was quick to respond, "The mischievous vulture has turned your mind! Has he not deluded you with his cunning arguments and convinced you with his glib talks! Now I realize how false your love is for your own flesh and blood! Remember, one should not give up hope. The God in the heavenly skies and your efforts here on earth may work miracles. Do not give into frustration. You should wait till the sun sets down fully or wait here for some more time trying to revive the child."

The vulture replied, "I have lived for more than one thousand years, I have never seen any male, female or human coming back to life after his death."

The vulture said further, "Some die in the womb, some after birth, some in adolescence, and some others in the prime of youth. Even the fate of animals and birds is uncertain. The life of all moving and unmoving beings is limited by time. Everyday many people lose their dear and loved ones and spend days and nights in sorrow. Countless people have left here, their hundreds of relations and thousands of friends. This child can neither see, hear, touch or smell. Why do you wait for him? His dead body is now hard as dead wood. My words may sound harsh to you, but they are true and worthy of respect. I am full of wisdom and experience. I have knowledge that I impart to others. I teach others the truth of life and death. Leave all hope and go home. Do not prolong your misery."

Having heard these words from the vulture, the men prepared to move on the way to home.

The jackal saw this. He again quickly came near the body of the child. And he told them, "Friends, look at this child. His skin is shining as bright as gold. He is charming and decorated with gariands. How can you leave him here? You are getting misguided by the cruel vulture. The child may live, and bring name and fame to his father. Remember, there are many instances of dead people coming back to life. Have you forgotten a Brahmin's dead child came alive during the reign of King Rama. The son of the great King Sweta died in childhood, but he revived later. May be some great saints or sages or some kind god takes pity on you too and bestow new life on this child. Wait and watch."

These words of the jackal revived hope in the brahmin and his relatives. They came back near the dead child. The father put the child's head in his lap and began to cry loudly. This attracted the Vulture.

The vulture came closer to him and said, "Your tears have made your child's dead body wet. The pressure of your palm has made imprints on his corpse. Sages, wealthy persons, kings and queens all come to the end. Death has taken away hundreds and thousands of friends and relations. This is not a place of happiness. This is the city of spirits. It is foolish to wait and hope for the impossible. Go home! Nobody has returned from the clutches of death. If the gods, Lord Vishnu, Lord Shiva, God Kartikaya or Lord Brahma bestow blessings, only then he may come back to life. Your loud cries, tears and beating of the chest can be of no use. This jackal, you and I, all of us whatever we are, it is because of our own good or evil deeds in our past lives. Give up bad habits, enmity, jealousy, and exploitation of others. Show mercy to others and follow the right path. Better look after your living parents, and relatives, and friends. Leave him alone and go."

Again the relatives prepared to leave the body on the ground and go home. This disappointed the jackal and he said, "This mortal world is full of sorrow. Life is short. And happiness is ephemeral. I do not find here any merit. The world is full of falsehood. We find a lot of worthless speakers and preachers, but few who speak sweet but true words."

The jackal continued, "This vulture is cunning and sinful; His heart is full of malice. Do not believe him. Sorrow and happiness are like night and day. One follows the other. You are in sorrow so you may not see happiness coming. You should wait. Have firm faith in happiness, and strive with determination to achieve it. Do not stop your efforts like a coward."

The jackal was an old resident of that place. He wanted them to stay till the sun fully set and darkness prevailed, so that he could feed on the dead body. He stopped the relatives of the dead child with his illogical arguments, and cunning words. They were in a fix.

The vulture warned them, "This place is full of ferocious animals. The night will be dark. The trees are thick and dreadful. Lots of ghosts may appear. At least you can perform the ritual of offering water to the dead soul in the river near by. This is better done while the sun is in the sky. Do not delay! If you listen to the false arguments of this foolish jackal, you may all do a grave blunder by not performing the holy rituals."

The jackal retorted, "No, no. This vulture is misguiding you. Although this is a burial, place, this is a charming spot. No danger, no fear. The sun is quite bright, if you are afraid because of the words of the Vulture, you will lose your child. He is after all a flesh-eater."

The vulture and the jackal both were very hungry. They had their own interests. So they were talking accordingly. The vulture wanted them to go, so that he could feed on the body in the daylight. The Jackal, was delaying them to deprive the vulture, so that he could feast on the corpse in the darkness of the night.

The relatives were swayed by the equally weighty arguments the vulture and the jackal for a long time.

❑

The Golden Mongoose

Once, there was a great praise for a yajna performed by King Yudhishthira. He donated gold, jewellery, clothes, blankets and utensils generously. He also donated hundreds of cows along with golden pots to the priests at the yajna. The cows were decorated with rich ornaments.

All the kings and noble leaders of the common people enjoyed delicious feast, beautiful dancing damsels entertained them. Everybody's wish was fulfilled generously by the king.

This royal event was the talk of even distant lands. People spoke with high praises for King Yudhishthira. They all said that there had been no other yajna as worthy as King Yudhishthira's yajna. In future also no other king would be able to perform such a sacrifice. But after the sacrifice was over, a very strange event took place at the site of the yajna.

While the great scholars, the king's relatives, his friends, the blind, the invalid and the destitute were showering flowers and blessings on King Yudhishthira, a mongoose visited the place. Its eyes were blue. One side of its body was shining like gold. When the mongoose came to the venue of the yajna, there was a thunderous sound that made the animals and the birds afraid.

The mongoose spoke in a human voice to the people at the yajna, "Oh king, this sacrifice of yours is not equal to the sacrifice of a poor Brahmin who had donated only a kilo of barley flour."

All the great scholars assembled there, were very much surprised to hear this statement.

Now the Brahmin priests surrounded the mongoose and asked, "On this great yajna only worthy scholars have been invited. From where have you come here? What is your qualification? What do you know about the Holy Scriptures? Who are you to criticize our great ceremony? We have collected all the holy and pious items for this event. We have followed all the rules while performing this yajna."

The Brahmin priests continued, "Every ritual at this yajna has been performed properly and according to the direction of the scriptures. Revered persons have been honored. Mantras have been properly recited. Donations have been made without any hitch and hindrance. The king has donated various things to the priests. He has paid respect to elders. He has offered lifetime protection to the trading classes and has honored the women folk with gifts. He has been kind to the labouring classes and has spoken with every one with sweet words. He has offered protection to all his wards. In spite of all these things what makes you belittle the importance of this yajna? If you are a scholar yourself, you must give us an honest answer."

The mongoose smiled and said, "Oh Sir! I didn't lie. I do not talk in arrogance. I have already told you that this sacrifice is not equal to the sacrifice made by a poor Brahmin who just donated a kilo of barley flour. You have heard me correctly. Oh, scholars I will explain my statement. I request you to listen to my words carefully."

The mongoose said, "There was once a poor Brahmin in Kurukshetra. He lived with his wife, son and daughter-in-law. He used to feed his family by picking up left over grains from the fields after the harvest season. He was undergoing a great penance. Many times the whole family used to remain on fast. They never collected food for the next day.

Once, a great famine affected the area. It was the hot month of summer. For weeks the Brahmin and his family could not get food or water.

By chance one day, somehow the family could collect one kilo of barley. The poor family prepared the flour. They bathed and recited the mantras. They performed a small yajna and then divided the food equally in four parts.

But as they were about to sit for a meal, a guest appeared at their door. The poor Brahmin was happy to receive the guest. He enquired of his welfare and extended a hearty welcome to him. He said, "Sir here is water for you and here is a place to sit and here is the flour, which have been properly prepared. Kindly, accept this food and oblige us."

The guest was very happy to receive the warm welcome by the poor Brahmin. The guest took his share of flour and water and ate it up quickly. But his hunger was not satisfied and his thirst was not quenched.

So the wife of the host offered her share to the guest. She was herself lean and thin, her body was all bones because of fasting for many days. Her husband did not want her to give up her share and he said, "My dear, it is my duty to feed and protect you. You are already very weak, and you have been on a fast for many days. How can you offer your share?"

The wife replied, "You are everything to me. It is my duty to help you in serving our guest. You are also weak and lean, and have been on a long fast. If you could offer your share, why can I not do the same?"

Saying this she gladly handed over her share of the food to the guest. The guest quickly ate up her food. But his hunger was not satisfied. This made the host very sad.

The brahmin's son was also watching all this. Now he came forward to offer his share of the food. But the father was unwilling to accept the son's share of the food.

The son said, "It is my duty to help and support you. I am a bone of your bone and flesh of your flesh. I am young. I can live without food for many more days. Please accept my share, father, and give it to our guest."

"Dear son, even if you become a thousand year old, you will be, for me a child. I am old. Whether I live or die, does not matter. So it is I who should remain without food for many days," said the father.

But the son insisted on offering his share of the food to the guest. The brahmin finally took the son's share and offered that also to the guest. The guest quickly ate up the share. But he was still not satisfied.

This made the brahmin sad. Now his daughter-in-law came forward with her share of food. She said, "Sir, you are my husband's father. So you deserve my complete respect and honor. I have heard that a son or a grandson should keep the honor of the family. Kindly accept my share and offer it to the guest too."

The brahmin tried his best to dissuade his daughter-in-law. He said to her, "You are a young lady. How can I accept your share?" But the young daughter-in-law replied, "Sir, you are the god of my god, and the preceptor of my preceptor. Kindly accept my offer. Do not deprive me of my sacred duty. My life, my body, my every thing is for serving the elders."

The Brahmin host said, "You are a pious lady, I will not deprive you of the merit of this charity."

The Brahmin took her share also and offered it to the guest. The guest ate up the share quickly. Now he was fully satisfied.

But then the guest revealed his true identity. He was an incarnation of the god of Dharma. He said, "O poor Brahmin, your penance is perfect. You and your family have conquered hunger and anger, and achieved the control of your sense organs. The heavens are pleased with your sacrifice. They are showering flowers on you and your family."

The god of Dharma said, "Your charity is superb. Hunger kills intelligence and wisdom. It dries up religious feelings, it takes away our patience. But you have conquered this hunger. By doing so, you have conquered the heavens. The gods are eager to welcome you and your family."

"When this event was over," said the mongoose to his audience, "I ventured out of my abode under the earth. I smelled the particles of that food that the Brahmin and his family had offered to the guest. My body touched the mud in the house of the poor Brahmin and that portion of my body changed into golden colour. Since then, whenever I hear of some great sacrifical ceremony. I visit the place, rub my body against the mud of the place. I move about the ashrams of great hermits and palaces of mighty kings who are famous for their charity and penance. But till now the other half of my body has not changed into golden colour."

The mongoose further said, "When I heard the great fame of the yajna being performed by King Yudhishthira, I thought I could change my body into golden colour now by rubbing it against the mud of this place. O scholars, you may yourselves see. My skin has not changed. That is why I smiled and said that this great charity is not equal to the charity of the poor Bramhin's offer of one kilo of barley."

Having said this, the mongoose vanished from the palace. The host of scholars could not say anything. Hanging their heads low, they silently left for their homes.

❑

The Insect and Sage Vyas

One day the great scholar and sage Sri Vyas was travelling on a journey. On his way, he found a small insect running very fast on a cart track. Sage Vyas was omniscient. He could understand the language of insects, birds and beasts. He was very surprised to find the insect hurrying down the track. The insect was afraid and seemed to be rushing off with great speed.

The sage asked, "O! Dear insect, what makes you run so fast? Why are you so afraid?" The insect replied "O! Great sage a very heavy cart is coming right behind me. It is producing a fearful sound. I am very afraid. When I hear its loud noise, I apprehend it may crush me down. That is why I am running away so fast. Look, the cart driver is whisking the whip, so the bullocks carrying the heavy load of the cart are running toward me. The people sitting in the cart also talk very loudly. I want to only save my life."

The great scholar Sri Vyas said, "O! Insect, what happiness do you get in your life? I think it is better for you to die. You are born in the lowest grade of living creatures. You cannot enjoy the pleasures of music, touch, taste and smell? What is the use of your life?"

The insect smiled and replied, "O! Great wise man, living creatures enjoy happiness in all grades of life. I also enjoy happiness in my unworthy life. I would never want to give up my life. My body also enjoys certain pleasures. The pleasure of human beings and that of trees and plants are different from mine but that does not diminish the joys of my life.

O! Sage, in my previous life I was a man. I was very rich but I had no respect for scholars and saints. I was a miser and a usurer, cruel and unkind to all. My tongue was harsh and I used to cheat people with my lies.

I never fed the poor and the needy. Never gave protection to persons in trouble. I was also always jealous of others' happiness. That is why after death I was born in this birth as an insect. But in my previous birth I had done one good deed. Once when I was serving my mother I had also offered some food to a pious scholar. Because of that single meritorious deed, today, I have the ability and gift to remember the events of my previous life. Pray, tell me about the life of a pious person?"

The Great sage Vyas said, "O! Insect, because of sins committed in previous life, you have suffered and received the birth of an insect. It is good that you wish to know about the life of a pious person. You have faith in Dharma. I hope you achieve further happiness of life. Human beings and animals get a good or bad future according to their deeds performed in this world. This is Karma. Ignorant people perform duties only for the sake of fulfillment of desires. But a man, wise or foolish, devoid of speech, intelligence and limbs of the body cannot achieve much in life. I bless you, "O Insect! you will be born in a scholarly family as the son of a great scholar."

Having heard these words of blessing from the great sage Vyas, the insect stopped running to save its life. The heavy load of the cart came closer. It slowly passed over the body of the insect. The insect was crushed to pieces. The insect took birth in several species in quick succession after that and ultimately it was born in the family of a king. He remembered his previous birth as an insect.

When he was a king, he went to the great sage Vyas and said, "O Sage! it is because of your blessings that I have been born in a royal clan after having lived a menial life of a small insect. Today, I am carried by big elephants decorated with garlands of gold. High-bred horses are yoked to my chariot and I enjoy delicious food and drinks along with my relatives and ministers. I sleep on a cushioned bed in a beautiful palace. Musicians, poets and great scholars sing songs in my praise. You are pious and sacred so you have transformed me from an insect into a prince. I bow to you. I want to serve you. So tell me what can I do for you?"

The great Vyas said, "O! Prince I do not need any personal favour from you, nor do I need your wealth. I only want you to protect the great scholars and the subjects under you with great care and love. That will be true service to me."

The prince bowed before the knowledgeable sage and went back to his kingdom.

❑

The Pigeon and the Hunter

Once there lived a cruel hunter in a dense forest. He was a very mean person. His looks were dreadful and sinister. He was the very incarnation of evil. His body was as dark as a witch's raven. His eyes were small, he had a monstrous face, and a distorted chin.

Due to his evil nature and cruelty, the hunter's brothers, friends and relatives had forsaken him. So he lived in the forest in the company of his wife. Every day the hunter would go into the deep forest with his nets and snare to catch some animals. He did not like to do any other work.

One day while the hunter was moving about in the deep forest, there came a big storm. The speed of the wind was so great that it seemed to bend all the trees to the ground. The sky was overcast with dark grey clouds and a torrential rain flooded the whole area. It became so cold that the hunter started to shiver. He soon lost his sense of direction and was utterly lost in the dark forest. The storm killed a large number of birds and beasts and injured many. Some of these gentle creatures were floating lifeless in the water and other lay still in their nests and abodes. Those who could survive were seeking shelter in hordes. The hunter was cold and tired. He could neither stand erect nor walk steadily on his feet. As he tottered along the jungle path, he spotted an injured she-pigeon, lying on the ground. She was also suffering from the bitter cold.

The hunter scooped up the injured bird in his arms and put it into his cage. He walked along till he saw a big green tree. The tree was a favourite abode of a large number of birds that came there for relief, residence and fruits.

Soon the hunter saw the sky darkening. The clouds scattered, the stars began to twinkle like white flowers in a big blue lake. The hunter's hut was very far from where he stood. So he decided to spend the night under the same tree. He spread some leaves on a flat rock and lay down there. He placed the cage with the she-pigeon nearby.

On the same tree a he-pigeon had been living since long with his family. He was in his nest just above where the hunter lay fast asleep. His wife had gone in search of food. She had not yet returned to the nest. The he-pigeon was very sad and lamenting." It is such a terrible storm and raining so heavily too! My beloved wife has not returned. I am worried for her welfare. Without her, my home is lifeless. I pray that she is safe. A house is not a house without the wife. My beloved has beautiful eyes. Her sound is sweet music. How can

I live if she does not return tonight? She is a pious creature. She has never taken even a morsel of food without first serving me food. My happiness used to thrill her, my sadness used to make her sad. When I was angry, she talked to me sweet words and soothed my feelings. When I came back to the nest tired, she looked after me. She was helpful to me when I was in trouble or in an alien land. It is a wise saying, 'Even a big palace without a wife is as fearful as a dark forest.' If a man has no loyal and sweet-speaking wife in his house he should live in a forest."

The she-pigeon, for whom the he-pigeon was lamenting atop the tree, was in the hunter's cage. She was glad to hear her praises. "I do not know whether I possess these virtues he is singing about. But he is my respected husband. A woman must be loyal to her husband. She cannot have the worldly happiness and the heavenly blessings without her husband. It is her obligation to keep her husband happy."

The she-pigeon was extremely miserable in the cage and she found her husband also sad and miserable. She spoke to him, "My dear, I seek to advise you for your good. Listen to me and do accordingly. You have a poor guest at your house and you must protect him. This hunter has come to your door. He is suffering from hunger and cold and lying on the ground. Give him shelter. You are a pious house-holder. It is your duty to provide for the guest as much as you can. You have begotten many children and tasted all sorts of food and drink. Do not bother for your bodily comforts. It is time now to earn religious virtues by sacrifice. So, please extend such welcome provisions to the hunter too so that he is comforted and satisfied. Do not worry for me that I am in a cage. You may find another wife if you so like." Having spoken thus, the pious she-pigeon kept looking hopefully at her husband on the tree above.

The pigeon heard the wise and virtuous words of his wife. He was overjoyed and tears of happiness rolled down his eyes. The hunter was a cruel killer of birds. He was a habitual enemy of the winged clan. Yet, the he-pigeon extended a warm welcome to him. He spoke, "Today I welcome you, tell me, what can I do for you. Do not worry; you are in your own house. Now tell me quickly whatever you wish me to do. You are my honorable guest. One should welcome even one's enemy, if he comes to his door. The tree extends shade even to that person who comes to cut it down. Everybody should extend a warm welcome to a guest, but it is the supreme duty of a householder in particular. Have full faith in my hospitality. And tell me whatever you wish me to do. I am totally at your disposal."

Having heard these sincere words, the hunter replied, "At present I am suffering from severe cold. Please devise some means to protect me from this unbearable chill."

The bird readily collected some leaves and gathered them near the tree. It flew to a village-smith's oven, and picked up a burning ember from there. The ember was enough to ignite the leaves. The bird requested the hunter to warm himself near the burning fire. Sitting near the bonfire, the hunter was happy and comforted with new warmth of life. At the same time the hunter was also overwhelmed to find such a generous welcome and his eyes brimmed with tears of gratitude. He looked at the pigeon. The hunter addressing the bird said, "Brother, I am grateful to you but I am also suffering from severe pain of hunger. I want some food. Don't you have any food for me?"

The bird replied, "Brother, I do not have food stored in my house to satisfy your hunger. We are forest birds, we search for food everyday. We do not store or gather food for the next day. Like the forest-dwelling sages we do not store food for the future." Having said this the bird was sad. He thought and thought. What was the way out? He repented his inability to satiate the hunter's hunger. He consoled the hunter and requested him to wait. "I will think of some way to satisfy your hunger," said the he-pigeon.

It again ignited the leaves and said, "There is no virtue greater than properly welcoming a guest. I have decided to follow the path of supreme duty. You can satisfy your hunger with the flesh of my body." Saying this, bird jumped into the burning fire.

The hunter was stunned and dumbfounded. He saw the bird in the fire and cried, "Oh! What have I done with this pious creature? This gentle bird did not even know me. Yet it accorded a welcome fit for a king to a stranger. Unknowingly this little pigeon has taught me a lesson. From now on I will also be kind and good to all living creatures. I will mend my ways. I will give up my bad profession and seek to do something else. As the hunter said this, his face lost its mean look. He looked humane. The hunter slowly opened the door of the cage and let the she-pigeon fly away."

❑

The Story of a Swan and a Crow

Once, there was a prosperous businessman who lived in a port town. He was very liberal and gave alms to a large number of poor people every day. He had many children.

These children used to go to the seashore and feed a crow with rice, curd and other eatables everyday. The crow grew fat and bold and began to look down upon his kith and kin, and birds of other inferior species. He began disregarding even the superior bird species.

Once, a large number of swans that could fly long stretches of distance like Garud, came to the seashore. The arrogant crow came to them and said, "Come, let us have a flying competition."

The newly arrived swans heard this and burst into laughter. They replied to the bragging crow, "We are swans from the Mansarovar and we fly to all corners of the earth. Because of our ability to fly long distances all other birds show respect to us. Brother, you are just a crow, why do you challenge swans! Tell me, how can you compete in flying with us?"

The crow's pride was hurt. He replied, curtly and started to brag about his strength. He showed off his knowledge of the art and science of flight.

The crow said, "I know one hundred and one ways of flying. Each variety of flight may last for hundreds of kilometres each. They are all strange acrobatic exercises in the air."

For a long time the crow described dozens types of flights before the swans. He asserted that he could display those flights in their presence too.

The clever swans wanted to see and find out how strong the crow really was. Soon the crow asked them, "Now tell me which flight you would like me to show, and at what speed?"

One of the swans then came forward and said, "O Crow, surely you might know more than a hundred variety of flights. But other birds only have one style. I will fly in my simple style in a competition against you. I do not know any other style. You may choose any style you like." This made his companion swans laugh.

They said to each other, "How can this swan with the knowledge of only one style of flight compete with one who knows more than a hundred styles?"

The crow and the swan were soon ready to participate in the competition. The crow was displaying a variety of acrobatics in the sky. This amazed the onlookers. The swan had only one style. The crow was very fast, but the swan was comparatively slower.

When the crows saw this, the onlookers made disparaging comments, "Look, the swan has started flying. But he is too slow for the crow!"

The swan heard this and he gradually increased his speed and started flying toward the western sea. He flew and flew over the vast sea and the crow was soon very tired.

As the crow continued to fly in competition with the swan, no island or tree was visible to him to take rest. He was filled with fear. He apprehended, "I may get so tired and exhausted that I may fall down into the sea."

Ultimately, tired and exhausted, the crow approached the swan. The swan noticed the crow's miserable state and asked, "Hello, my friend, you described hundreds of styles of flights, but you kept this style a secret. What is this style in which you dip your beak and wings again and again in the sea water?"

Now the crow said, "Dear Brother Swan! I am just a crow. It is the habit of a crow and his brothers to indulge is false bragging. I surrender before you. Kindly save me and take me out of this water to the sea shore."

Having spoken this, the exhausted crow fell into the sea. The swan replied, "You were proud of your hundred and one style flights. How is it that now you are in the water?"

The miserable crow spoke in agony, "O Swan, I was fed on leftovers. I grew fat and arrogant, and considered myself superior to even Garud, the most powerful of all birds. I have shown disrespect to many crows and other birds too. But now, I am at your mercy. Save me. Kindly take me to some island or back to the seashore. If somehow I reach my own country, I will not show disrespect to any one ever again. Have pity on me."

The crow was now sobbing and almost unconscious. His pitiable condition moved the kind-hearted swan. He came to the crow, lightly held him with his claws and gradually pushed him up onto his own back.

Then he flew back to the place from where they had started the flying competition. He put the crow down on the earth and nursed him. Later that day the swan returned to his herd and left with his brothers for another long flight to the Himalayas.

❑

The Dove and the King

Once there lived a famous king in Kashi. His name was Ushinar. One day King Ushinar was sitting on his golden throne, and discussing the state's affairs with his courtiers. All of a sudden, a dove fell into his lap. The bird was gravely injured. Its wings were damaged and its body was bleeding. A fierce hawk had attacked it.

The king looked at the dove with pity and compassion. His heart welled up with I the milk of kindness.

He began to console the dove and assure him of full protection. He said, "O Dove, calm down, fear no more. Where from did you come? What danger did you face? What harm have you done to your adversary? You are a charming bird. Your eyes are as red as blood. I must save you, even at the cost of my life and my kingdom. Believe me and calm down now."

When the king was thus assuring the dove, a hawk arrived there. It had been pursuing its prey, the dove. The hawk told the king, "Sir, God has allotted this bird as my food. Now that I have caught it, its life is over.

Do not extend your protection to it. I have searched for it with great difficulty. Its blood, flesh, marrow and intestine are healthy food for me. I am hungry and thirsty. This dove will satisfy my hunger. Please do not interfere and obstruct my pursuit. I have been chasing it for quite a long time and have flown after it for a long distance. Now it is on the verge of death. Leave it for me."

The hawk looked at the king and continued, "Sir, you are a king. It is your duty to protect your subjects. You have been appointed a ruler to protect human beings. You have no control over the sky and the birds.

If you want to do your duty, protect your servants, subjects and fight to vanquish your enemies. If you try to protect this dove for the sake of religious merit, you must take my hunger also into consideration."

The king was greatly dismayed at hearing the arguments of the hawk. With a view to save the life of the dove, the king said, "O hawk, if you leave this poor dove; you may be provided with the flesh of other animals. Such as bull, buffalo, pig or stag. I cannot give up this dove, which has come under my protection. This is my vow, not to forsake anyone who seeks my care and shelter. Look, this poor bird is quivering with fear, and clinging to my body."

"O King," said the hawk, "I cannot accept the flesh of a bull, buffalo, pig or stag. They are not my natural food. What will I do with them? The whole world knows that God has allotted birds for my food. This has been so from the beginning of Creation.

O King, if you love this dove so much, I have no objection! You may barter your own flesh for the amount of the flesh of the dove."

The king readily agreed and said, "O hawk I am very grateful to you." Then the king ordered for a weighing machine to be brought there. He began carving out flesh from his thigh, arms, chest and put it on the weighing machine. But the flesh would not equal the weight of the dove.

The king was greatly surprised. There was a great commotion in the palace. Beautiful queens, relatives of the king and courtiers all gathered at the court. The royal women began weeping and crying. Servants and dependents were astonished. When the king found that his flesh was not equal to the weight of the dove he stood up, and him self went and sat on the weighing machine.

The sky was then suddenly overcast with clouds. It is said that gods appeared in the sky, and sang the glory of the king who was prepared to make supreme sacrifice to protect the life of a mere bird.

Till today, people believe the hawk and the dove were no other than gods who had come to test King Ushinar.

❑

The Poor Scholar and the Wise Jackal

Once there was a great scholar who was very poor and slothful. One day he decided to go to a town in search of some work. While he was walking towardthe town, a rich young businessman was driving his chariot on the same road. His horses were running swiftly. The rich businessman did not care for the poor scholar walking along on the road. As he drove past, the poor man was pushed by the rich man's speeding chariot. The scholar tumbled and fell down on the dusty road. The arrogant businessman did not care to stop to help or console the scholar. He kept onward on his journey non-stop.

Somehow the poor man got up staggering back on his feet. His legs and hands were bruised. There were injuries at several places on his body. He was very sad and angry. He said aloud to himself, "Now I will commit suicide. No misery is greater than poverty. The life of a poor man is worthless. This rich businessman had no care for my safety. Such is my worthless life!"

Speaking so, the scholar took out a piece of cloth and decided to hang himself by a roadside tree.

By chance there appeared a jackal before the poor scholar. When the jackal found the poor man set on ending his life, he said, "Why do you look so sad and want to end your life? You are a human being. The life of a human being is far superior to any other form of life. You are lucky that you are born in a family of pundits. You are yourself a great scholar of the Vedas. You know that self-killing is a great sin. Then how can you think of doing so?"

"All the worldly gains make humans only proud and vain. God has created you to have control over your greed. God has given you two hands. As a human being you must use your hands only, to acquire wealth. Animals are different. We consider your "hands" as a great gift of God."

'No gift is greater than these hands, O Brahmin. Sometimes thorns pierce our body. But we have no hands to pull them out. Mosquitoes and bugs bite us and we cannot ward them off. Men with ten fingers can protect themselves from bugs and mosquitoes and other enemies. They wear cloth, eat food, and spread a bed to sleep and rest comfortably. Men with hands move on carts, and use them in various ways. They use their hands to control other animals and birds and other men. As a man you do not have to suffer the problems, which weak animals without hands have to face. You are indeed lucky. It is your great good luck that you were not born as a jackal or rat or frog or snake or some insect. You should thank God and feel grateful that you are born as a human being, and in a scholar class."

"Look, even though this insect bites me, I cannot cast it away. Committing suicide is a heinous crime and extremely sinful, so I do not discard this body of mine. I fear that if I do so I may be born in a more inferior species. At least my present body of a jackal is superior to many others."

"Some species and gods are happy by birth while others like animals suffer untold miseries. But I do not find superior living beings always in happiness. I have seen that when a man becomes wealthy, he desires to gain some kingdom. Then he desires to become powerful like gods. The gods are also always suffering from want. They all aspire for the post of Indra, the ruler of gods."

"Look at your own life, O Brahmin. You may be rich, but you cannot be a ruler, because you are a Brahmin. By chance, if you become a ruler, you may not be a god. Even if you become a god and even Indra, you will not remain contented with that. The gain of pleasant things does not quench your thirst for more. The lust grows more each day. The fire blazes more if you put more fuel into it. Your heart always has both sadness and happiness. Then what is the use of only lamenting? The sense organs and the intellect are the root cause of our desires and actions. If you keep them caged like a bird, under control, there is no problem. A man is never afraid of losing his second head or third hand. There is no problem because there is no fear in loss of a non-existent thing. If you do not know the taste of a thing, you do not crave for that. Craving comes from touching, hearing and looking at a material thing."

"You are a Brahmin. May be you have not tasted wine or meat, so you may not have lust for them. But a person who has tasted them will pine for them. I consider it a great merit to abstain from the use of the pleasant things, which lure the sense organs."

"He alone is really wealthy and powerful who has two healthy hands. Men are enslaved by men themselves. Many people suffer imprisonment and atrocity. But they do not commit suicide. They rejoice and laugh together. Many others are bestowed with knowledge, wisdom and strength, but spend miserable sinful and slothful life. Many are crippled, without legs and hands. Some paralyzed, many are lifelong invalids. You look quite hale and hearty. Your limbs are strong and healthy. You are lucky to have a healthy human form. No one can laugh at or pity you."

"There is no deformity in you. Even if you have been severely criticized or despised for some misconduct, there is no reason for you to die. Gird up your loins and arise for the battle of life, for the performance of your duty (Dharma). If you listen to me and act accordingly, you will achieve the meritorious career of a Vedic scholar."

"Be careful; practice self-study, control of desire, control of sense organs, and faith in the Supreme Lord. You are a Brahmin; you must perform your duties as assigned to your class. Use your hands and your intellect; face the problems of the world with courage and determination."

Having spoken so the jackal said, "In previous life, I was a pundit (scholar). With logic and arguments I used to demolish the Vedic precepts. In meetings and seminars I used to emphasize on the efficacy of my ideas. I was an atheist always ridiculing others. That is why in this life I was born as a jackal. Have faith in the Supreme Lord and fight the battle of life with determination."

The poor Brahmin took heart. He was inspired by the wisdom of the jackal. He said, Sir, you are very wise and intelligent. You cannot be a beast. You must be some god perior spirit to appear here for my good fortune. Thank you for your advice, you are my guru now."

Thereafter the Brahmin gave up slothfulness and pessimism. He decided to live and do his duty as a human being. He returned to his village, his home and with vigour and enthusiasm began a new phase of life.

❑

Lord Indra and the Parrot

Once, there was a hunter in the land of Kashi. He used to hunt with arrows tipped with poison. One day with his bow and arrows he set out from his village to hunt in the forest. In a remote place of the forest he saw some deer grazing in the field. He shot at them his poisonous arrows, one after another. But his arrows lissed their mark. The deer ran away.

One of the arrows pierced a big tree very hard. The poison spread through the tree. The leaves, flowers and fruits of the green tree began to rot and fall. Soon the tree turned into a dried wooden structure.

There was a small hole in the tree. A parrot had made this tree-hole its home. He had lived in it right from birth. The parrot was very attached to the tree, so even when it was dead wood now, the parrot did not leave the hole. He was very sad. He gave up food and drink. After some time, he became so weak that he could not even chirp. Along with the tree, the bird was also dying day-by-day. His loyalty to the tree was miraculous. The bird showed exemplary equanimity with the tree, in happiness and misery.

The strange behaviour of the parrot moved Lord Indra. It was unnatural for a bird to stick to a decaying tree. So Indra came down from the heavenly skies to the tree, and took the form of a human being.

Indra said to the parrot, "O, noble parrot, your family is proud of you. But tell me, why do you stick to the dead wood, and injure yourself?"

The parrot bowed its head respectfully and answered, "Sir, I know you are Lord Indra. You are welcome to my home. I can identify you, because of my power of penance."

Lord Indra appreciated the intelligence of the parrot. But he kept silent. He again asked, "O bird, the tree has lost its leaves. There are no fruits on it any more. It is not fit as an abode and shelter for birds. The vast forest is standing before you. Why do you stick to this naked wood? The vast forest has innumerable trees covered with green leaves; they have enough space for shelter of birds. O bird, this tree's life is over. It has lost its sap and its beauty is gone. You should ponder over what I am saying and give up its company."

The parrot heard these words, and felt sad. With great pain he replied, "Sir, I was born in this tree, I learnt a lot of good things here. The tree protected me as its own child and warded off attack of my enemies. So I am loyal to this tree. I have decided to remain along with it, at the time of its adversity You of all the holy Gods, should not dissuade me from this meritorious duty. When Gods have doubts about their duty, they ask you for guidance. That is why you enjoy the post of Indra. Great souls must help others in trouble. Kindness fills the world with happiness."

The parrot continued woefully, "Please, do not try to separate me from this tree. When it was capable, it protected me for long years. I was nourished by it. Now that it is weak and suffering, then how can I desert it? How is it possible?"

Lord Indra was greatly pleased with the reply of the bird. He was highly impressed with the firmness of loyalty of the kind-hearted parrot. He asked the parrot to ask for a boon. The parrot asked, "Sir if you are pleased with me, then make this tree lush green with leaves, flowers and fruits again. I want nothing more than this."

Lord Indra sprinkled some nectar drops, and the tree stood just as it was before. It grew new, tender leaves and attractive branches with flowers and fruits.

❑

Pujanee and Brahmadutta

In very ancient times, there was a famous city called Kampilya. King Brahmadutta was the ruler of the city. In the interiors of his palace, a bird named Pujanee had been living in her nest for a long time. She had the miraculous gift to understand and speak the languages of various living creatures.

Once, the bird gave birth to a little fledgling in the palace. By chance, the queen of King Brahmadutta also gave birth to a bright charming son on the same day. The bird was loyal to the king. Every day, she used to fly to the shore of the sea, and pick up two fruits, one for her child and another for the king's son. The fruits brought by her were as sweet as nectar and very nutritious. The fruit made the little baby bird and the king's son healthy and strong. The prince grew very quickly because of the fruit.

One day, the nurse was strolling in the palace gardens with the prince. Suddenly the prince caught hold of the little bird and started playing with it. After sometime he took the little bird in a corner and killed it. Then he went to his nurse and sat in her lap.

When Pujanee returned with the fruits, she found her little baby lying dead. She knew that the prince had killed her little one. The little bird's body was lying torn into pieces on the ground. Pujanee was overwhelmed by sorrow. She cried bitterly.

"A king does not know how to maintain friendship. He has neither love nor affection. He deals with people only in self-interest. When his purpose is served, he throws even his dependents away. One should never trust a king. The prince is equally ungrateful, cruel and a betrayer. I must teach him a lesson, and take revenge. The two were born together, they used to play and eat together, and yet, the prince killed my child."

With these words, Pujanee dashed her claws into the eyes of the prince and damaged them.

There was great hue and cry in the palace. The queen, the servant, the guards all ran into the garden. The king also arrived quickly. He saw the plight of his crying son, and the bird. He readily grasped the situation, and controlled his anger. He knew that the bird had avenged the death of her issue.

Pujanee was preparing to leave the palace for good. But the king did not want the bird to go. He said, "We did commit a crime against you, and you have taken revenge. Now it is on par. You need not leave this palace. Stay here."

Pujanee, the bird said, "Sir, I have also committed a crime. Now that you have been harmed by my actions, it is not safe for me to stay here. The loss of your son's eyes will always rankle in your heart. I will also always be suspicious. I cannot be at ease anymore living in this palace. Once, I was greatly honored here, but now it is not possible to get that respect. I must leave this palace at the earliest."

The king again said, "The crime committed by you, is the payment made for the crime done to you. You are no more a criminal. You need not go away from here."

The bird replied, "I have committed an act of enmity. You may pardon it. But it will not be wise of me to get assured of safety here. Sometimes, sweet words are just a false cover. Even strong elephants are made captive by sweet words."

The king said, "O Bird, even ferocious persons become friends if they live together. If enemies live together, enmity vanishes, as water can not stay long on the leaf of the lotus."

The bird said, 'Sir, enmity grows because of six factors. Wise men know these six factors, which cause enmity. These six factors are women, house or land, harsh words, racism, hostility, and old injuries. One should not believe in a person, on whom harm has been inflicted. His anger is hidden, like fire in the wood. The fire of anger cannot be quenched by money, sweet words or by revenge. It cannot subside without finishing one party. Till now I did no harm to you; you did no harm to me, so, I was living here happily. Now I cannot have confidence in you."

The king said, "O Pujanee, time alone heals everything. All sorts of events take place because of time. We are not responsible. Birth and Death keep going on uninterrupted. Some people die in groups, many die one by one. You are not responsible for the injury of my child. I assure you, have no fear. Stay here gladly. I pardon you for whatever you have done."

"Sir!" said Pujanee, "If time alone is the agent of good and bad, why do people avenge the death of their near and dear ones? Why did the gods and demons fight several battles? Why do the doctors give medicine and treatment to patients? I have damaged the eyes of your son, you may kill me. Men catch birds either for food or for game. There is no other reason. Every species love its progeny, life is dear to all. Death is a cause of sorrow. Old age is sorrow; loss of wealth and contact with undesirable brings sadness. Loss of dear ones makes us unhappy. Sometimes enmity continues for many generations."

"O! Bird!" the king said, "the world is based on mutual trust and confidence. One cannot achieve anything without trust in others. If one is distrustful towards everybody, one's life will be miserable, forget the past and have confidence and trust again."

"O king, if your legs are injured and you try to run with them even cautiously, you may get hurt again and again," said Pujanee, "One should not rely on Time, Fate, Nature etc."

"One must use and believe in one's own intellect. Men have natural friends, knowledge, boldness, alertness, strength and patience. Wise persons rely on these trusted factors. A palatial house, precious metals, land, wife and relatives are only secondary factors. One may get them anywhere; I have no attachment to this place now. One should leave even one's birth place, if it is suffering from famine and pestilence. I cannot stay here any more. It is wise to say good bye to a bad ruler, infidel, wife and a disobedient son, a greedy friend and a bad country."

"One should never live under a hostile ruler. Sir, you know the qualities of a good king. If a weak person has brought on a quarrel with a mighty power, his destruction is only a matter of time. O, Sir, thank you very much for your sweet words. But I cannot live in this palace any more," Saying so Pujanee left the palace of King Brahamadutta for good.

❑

The Raven and the Rishi

In the ancient past, King Kshemdarshi ruled over the country of Koshal. King Kshemdarshi had a patron saint. The name of saint was Kaakvrikshiya. The saint was a great scholar of politics and administration. He was a great diplomat also.

Once, King Kshemdarshi was defeated in a battle. He lost his army and he had no money to raise a new battalion of soldiers either. The king's advisors and ministers also deserted him. The king was very sad and disheartened.

He went to meet the great saint at his humble hut. He stood before the saint and bowed before him. The king requested the saint to guide him so that he could regain his wealth, kingdom and friends.

He told him that he could neither commit suicide nor surrender, or want to take resort to any unethical methods. The saint put up certain questions before King Kshemdarshi.

With the king's answers, the saint came to the conclusion that he was a large-hearted person. He would always use his power and authority for the welfare of his subjects.

Judging so, the pious saint decided to give the young king proper advice.

The saint told the king, "O king, some people even without wealth, continue to live and some of them even manage to regain their lost glory. Some may be equal to you in intelligence and valour. Some kings who have lost everything also do not pine for what is lost. O King, whatever is left with you should be enough to lead a pious life. So do not be so unhappy."

Ultimately the saint described to the king the way to regain his kingdom. The king assured the saint that he would follow his guidance.

King Janak of Mithila was a friend of the saint. The saint advised King Kshemdarshi to approach King of Mathila for protection. He told him that the king of Mithila was a saintly person.

After a few days King Janak arrived in the forest to seek the blessings of Sage Kaakvrikshiya. In course of the talk the sage spoke very highly about the King of Koshal and requested King Janak to take him under his protection. In due course the young king called on King Janak. King Janak was impressed by his wisdom and large heartedness.

The king married his daughter to the young king, Kshemdarshi and gave him a large sum of money, gold, jewels and other costly gifts.

Very soon, the King of Koshal regained his kingdom and became a powerful ruler.

King Kshemdarshi was a wise and brave ruler. But he had one flaw. He gave free reign to his ministers and officers. He did not supervise the affairs of the kingdom personally. So slowly his ministers and officers started abusing their offices.

Now, sage Kaakvrikshiya had a peculiar habit. He kept a strange raven as pet. The sage often told people, "Gentle people you should learn the language of the raven. I have learnt this. The raven tells me everything about the present, past and the future."

When the sage came to know the corruption prevailing in King Kshemdarshi's kingdom, he began moving from place to place with his bird in a cage. This bird had miraculous powers. It could easily find out the cases of bribe, nepotism, and torture committed by the government officials.

The bird reported its findings to the sage, as they walked the length and breadth of King Kshemdarshi's kingdom. The sage was very sad. He went to the capital town to meet the king.

The king was surrounded by many ministers and high officers. They were all surprised to see the sage with his raven standing in the court. The sage was very blunt and frank. In the very presence of the king he charged his corrupt officers. He gave the details how and where they had committed the crimes.

The sage also told the king, "Your corrupt officers are torturing your poor subjects. They are indulging in unfair practices. This is not good either for you or for the kingdom. As your well-wisher, I want to advise you. You must look after affairs of the state yourself. A king, who does not keep vigilance, is easily destroyed by conspirators and enemies. Your kingdom is covered by dark clouds. Nobody is safe in your kingdom. The good and bad are being treated on equal footing. It is high time that you take stern measures to set things in proper order."

The king listened to the sage's advice respectfully. Having said everything, the sage wanted to leave the court, but the king offered hospitality. The sage agreed to stay in the king's palace for sometime.

King Kshemdarshi dismissed the court and went to his private chamber in the palace.

Next day the king came to his court. He was sitting in his throne when again sage Kaakvrikshiya came to his court. The saint was very sad. He said, "O king, you are surrounded by vicious enemies. They are living in your palace itself. They may plan to rebel against you. You are living in a house full of snakes. My raven has been keeping a watch and reporting their deeds."

The sage continued, "The conspirators even planned to kill me. They tried to use sharp deadly arrows to shoot me down. But their aim missed the target. My faithful raven was killed in the bargain. I was saved by chance. Now I cannot stay in your palace any longer."

The king was stunned to hear the saint. He said, "No, no, I must find out and punish the culprits. You should not leave the palace."

The sage said, "O king, Politics is a river, full of crocodiles and snakes in the guise of ministers and officers. Because of these rogues, no decent person can live in safety. The cunning culprits enjoy all comforts, and honest people face humiliation and danger to life. I am your well-wisher. Because of this, your corrupt officers have become hostile to me. They are now like poisonous reptiles that have been injured. I do not wish to stay here any longer."

The king assured the sage, "I will ward off all dangers and troubles. I will protect you. These conspirators and troublemakers will be eliminated. Those who plan to kill you will be punished. I will crush them. I request you to help me run the government in the best interest of my people."

The saint said, "O king, without announcing the names of the conspirators, you should divest them of their powers one by one. Then find out details of the conspiracy and put their lives to an end. When a similar charge is leveled against many persons, they form groups. Their unity becomes stronger and more powerful. They can create endless troubles for a king. That is why I advise you to put your traitors to death one by one. I do not want you to invite further trouble."

The sage said, "This kingdom of yours cannot be left in the care of only the ministers and officers. If you promise to take interest in the details of the functioning of the government, only then will I stay here. You are well aware that I have always been faithful friend to your father. After his death when you faced political upheavals. I again did everything possible to keep your kingdom safe."

"Now your kingdom is suffering from neglect. Internal and external enemies and conspirators are having free run. I again advise you to be fully vigilant, and active. Only then you can work in the interest of the state and the people and dharma," cautioned the sage.

King Kshamedarshi followed the sound advice about statecraft as propounded by Sage Kaakvrikshiya. He learnt from his mistakes and became stronger and more powerful. His name, fame and wisdom spread to distant lands.

❑

The Lazy Camel

Long, long ago there lived a camel. He was very pious. He could remember the events of his past life. Once he started on a course of hard penance. The Lord was moved by his arduous self-control. He appeared before him and proposed to grant him a boon.

The camel thought and thought over what to ask for. After a long serious mental exercise he said, "Lord, I am thankful to you for your kindness. I want the capacity to stretch my neck to become as long as hundred kilometres so that I do not have to walk in search of food for long distances." The Lord granted him this boon and disappeared.

The camel was very happy. He stopped further performance of penance. He went to the old forest where he used to live. Now he left making any attempts to search grazing grounds. He could stretch his neck for kilometres and kilometres wherever he wanted. He was no longer satisfied with grazing, his mouth watered for richer foods.

One day the camel had stretched his neck over a very long distance. His mouth entered into a long cave.

There in, he found delicious fodder. The camel was enjoying the delicious feast when suddenly clouds gathered into the sky and a heavy downpour flooded the forest.

In the heavy rain, a jackal and his wife were in search shelter. The two entered in to the cave. They were very hungry. So they attacked the neck of the camel and bit-by-bit they started feeding on the flesh of the camel. When the camel felt the jackals eating at his flesh, he felt great pain. He tried to pull back his neck from the cave but he could not do so. The jackal ate more and more of the camel's flesh.

The lazy camel died on the spot.

❑❑❑